Michele Jamal graduated ... anthropology from the University of California, Berkeley. She lives with her son in Fairfax, California, where she is working on another book. Arkana also publish her book *Shape Shifters: Shaman Women in Contemporary Society*.

MICHELE JAMAL

Volcanic Visions

ARKANA

ARKANA

Published by the Penguin Group
Penguin Books Ltd, 27 Wrights Lane, London W8 5TZ, England
Penguin Books USA Inc., 375 Hudson Street, New York, New York 10014, USA
Penguin Books Australia Ltd, Ringwood, Victoria, Australia
Penguin Books Canada Ltd, 10 Alcorn Avenue, Toronto, Ontario, Canada M4V 3B2
Penguin Books (NZ) Ltd, 182–190 Wairau Road, Auckland 10, New Zealand

Penguin Books Ltd, Registered Offices: Harmondsworth, Middlesex, England

First published 1991
1 3 5 7 9 10 8 6 4 2

Copyright © Michele Jamal, 1991
All rights reserved

The moral right of the author has been asserted

Filmset in Monophoto Bembo

Printed in England by Clays Ltd, St Ives plc

Except in the United States of America, this book is sold subject
to the condition that it shall not, by way of trade or otherwise, be lent,
re-sold, hired out, or otherwise circulated without the publisher's
prior consent in any form of binding or cover other than that in
which it is published and without a similar condition including this
condition being imposed on the subsequent purchaser

To my father, who showed me the road,
and to my friends on Hawaii
with whom I shared the journey

Mauna Loa

The mountain is a compass
that directs me to return
to a volcanic temple
of Lemuria past.
In my waking I remember
in my dreams I return
to the slopes
and feel the pounding
of my heart
as within me incense
rises from pikake flowers,
and magma flows down
in monthly streams.
On waking I remember and pray
to the womb mother,
I pray to the center
of myself.

CONTENTS

	Acknowledgements	xi
	Preface	xiii
1	Origins	1
2	The Calling	9
3	The Vog	17
4	Pele Mysteries	22
5	The Vision	26
6	Genesis	32
7	The Myth	40
8	The Script	49
9	Star Center	60
10	Acceleration	67
11	Walking on Coals	75
12	Volcanic Seeds	80
13	Numinous Places	84
14	Convergence	88
15	The Descent	99
16	Twilight	104
17	Retrospect	111
18	The Mythic Zone	115
19	Ring of Fire	122
	Epilogue	127
	Appendix	133
	Select Bibliography	135

Acknowledgements

My gratitude to the volcano goddess and the guardians whose energies inspired this book.

Many thanks to Herb Kane for the use of his stunning portrait of Pele on the cover.

My love and appreciation for my son, Josh, whom I dragged 3,000 miles across the ocean in pursuit of a vision.

Loving thanks to my mother, Anne, for her generous heart, and to my brother, Frank, whose insight helped me stay on the path.

And thanks to Jean Louis Brindamour, Dominie Capadonna and Marilyn Leese for encouraging me to publish my story.

A special thanks to my editor, Robin Waterfield, for his sensitivity and attunement to *Volcanic Visions*.

Preface

Volcanic Visions is about a quest to find and explore the metaphors and visions within me; discovering my mythology as it unfolded.

I first visited Hawaii in 1981 and, after returning to California, was haunted by dreams in which I flew back in my astral body to experience the islands again. Through the years I continued to feel a need to return to the Big Island, a yearning to be in an environment that is an inner and outer expression of my biological rhythms and psychic visions.

In 1987 Kilauea was erupting, as she had in the four previous years. Having completed writing *Shape Shifters*,* and no longer needing direct communication with the women I interviewed for the book, I sold my car and transported my son and myself to the Big Island. With just enough money to live frugally for six months, I went with a trust that I was being guided to some major shift and to experiences that would be integral to my spiritual awakening.

My intention was to interact with the environment, allowing myself to experience all the subtleties to which I could open. I wanted to be near the active volcano, perceiving my mood fluctuations, the effects of living near Pele, the volcano goddess. In her atmosphere and surroundings I wanted to kindle the flames within, and emerge with the awakening of my own primordial goddess, prophesying and speaking in tongues.

I had not expected that I would have visions and experiences that were on no map or itinerary that I created. I didn't know that I would find not only the mythology of the goddesses and gods of old Hawaii still alive today, but also a volcanic landscape steeped in extraterrestrial lore and consciousness. I wasn't expecting that mythic world to break in upon me.

---

*Michele Jamal, *Shape Shifters: Shaman Women in Contemporary Society*, London, Routledge & Kegan Paul, 1987.

Volcanic Visions

The move to the island was like a plunge into a mandala filled with archetypal images of power, for the island contains the core or seed of psychic integration in the fresh, hot, smoking magma flowing out of the Earth's belly. As Pele's fire crackles, her menstrual flow oozes into the sea and crystallizes into black jewels of sand, spawning millions of seeds from Pele's womb. The ocean surrounding Hawaii is populated with fish and sea animals with cosmic intelligence who hold wisdom secrets of ancient lands. Tropical palms come down to the sea, hanging coconuts in the sun, pregnant and full of milk. Waterfalls pour libations over the thick ferns, forming pools below, reflecting millennia of primal awareness, and orchids grow wild on the sides of trees and alongside of roads.

Being surrounded by jungle and volcanoes and thousands of miles of ocean created the sensation of living in a dream realm. The feeling was heightened by hearing tales of a secret land that rises out of the sea unexpectedly, and disappears as mysteriously. When driving on the northeast side of the island, I looked out over the turquoise sea and saw a distant mountain rise over the water ... Then it disappeared, like a phantom. What I saw was not a vision, but the top of the volcano Haleakala on Maui, visible on a cloudless day. Though not an apparition itself, the sight conjured up for me the specter of a resurrected world: Lemuria. And as central mysteries from the hidden realms of Mu appeared on the conscious horizon, I experienced the understanding of one who has moved aside the veil and touched each primordial form shimmering and infused with itself: a world pulsating and inseminated with mana.

In going to Hawaii I left behind me a four-sided mechanistic reality and entered another dimension. I turned to the fires of the volcano for salvation, and to the salty turquoise waters and the sultry blue skies. Volcanoes filled my dreams and my waking. Thought patterns, dreams and poetry became permeated with volcanic visions and pulsations.

When I wakened in the morning I knew whether volcanic activity had intensified during the night. It was in the smell of sulfur, and in the heaviness of the air. On one hand the fumes were oppressive; on the other, there was a feeling of being part of a primeval ritual in which we partook of the Earth's arousal, the Earth's passion and pungent breath. Eroticism permeated the island. For me it was hard on a psychic plane to live on a hot spot where the Earth is always aroused – always in heat. My reaction was to expand one moment, in orgasmic unity with the present, and to contract the next, in reaction to constant arousal overload.

To maintain some sort of balance between subjective inner worlds and the empirical outer plane, I created an archive. Daily, I logged references to volcanic eruption, and unusual occurrences on the island. I clipped out newspaper articles that cited locations for viewing lava flows, and events such as naming contests for new vents. I kept a medical advisory column for those sensitive to volcanic fumes, and weather predictions concerning levels of volcanic haze, or 'vog'. I cut out articles about the *kahuna* priests of the ancient Hawaiian religion and stories about the volcano goddess, fireballs and unidentified objects seen falling from the sky. Daily, I recorded my responses to living near an active volcano, and on an island whose legends assert that its earliest culture was created by people who came from the sky.

I came to Hawaii expecting the extraordinary, but I didn't realize how strong the undertow could be when penetrating the mythic zones. What I perceived inside became manifest outside, sometimes in the time it took to move from one thought to the next. I had come to a place where the interior life is accelerated and where the inner comes quickly into outer visual perception, like a hologram. It became harder and harder to distinguish between the linear, rational world and the subjective, visionary plane. I knew I was in danger when the volcanic fumes became too strong, the sea too filled with eels . . . visions too real.

When I spoke to my friends on the island about leaving, they said, 'It's too soon. It's too soon. Give it time. You will begin to understand. This is no ordinary place. You belong here.' My decision was made when my editor asked me to return to the mainland to promote *Shape Shifters*, which had just been published. It would be easier, I thought, to synthesize my experiences and psychic material in another place and the mainland would give me the necessary perspective. In the Bay area it is understandable to explore and study other realms of consciousness, but not so easy to slip into altered states just by breathing the atmosphere. Confirming to my friends our definite plans to leave Hawaii, I verbally slipped and said, 'When I leave this planet . . .'

On my return to California, I was still incubating inner mysteries and was not ready to drastically change gears, so I began to create a psychic bridge back to the islands. Through meditation I viewed the inner directives and mythic structure I had experienced there.

On the island, I had experienced an initial telepathic contact with invisible forces, which grew as a consciousness from an altered thought pattern. This experience expanded into dreams and channelings, and later manifested as visions and contact with my own mythology. The myths of Pele, the volcano goddess, and of Lemurian star-seed origins seemed to coincide with central motifs in my own psychic structure, and served as a catalyst to awaken past-life memories and images of a new direction.

In time, I became aware that the directives born of the inner world contained a psychic code and map, leading to creative productivity and new levels of spiritual awareness. After descending into the mythic inner world, it became necessary for me to make the ascent back into ordinary time, disseminating the crystals and pearls that I discovered there.

1

ORIGINS

*A salamander descending
into a burning cauldron
Emerging with its tail in mouth
tasting immortality*

There are many stories of how Pele, the fire goddess, came to Hawaii. She was born in the ancient homeland, which, according to some sources, was Tahiti. In one legend Pele's migration came about through a family dispute with her sister Namakaokahai, goddess of the sea, who was married to a great sorcerer. When he met Pele and her younger sister, Hi'iaka, he desired them as well, and secretly arranged to marry them. Discovering what her husband had done, Namakaokahai began to rage, creating tidal waves and floods that destroyed their homeland. In his concern, Pele's brother Kamohoali'i, the shark god, brought the rest of the family together to use their collective powers to oppose Namakaokahai. But the goddess of the sea drove them out to sea. Undaunted, the shark god created a large boat for his family to sail in in search of a new home far from Namakaokahai.

After many days they arrived at Hawaii, the lush home of the gods. They were overjoyed to find such a luxuriant place in which to settle. Pele immediately went looking for a place of power on which to build a new family home. From island to island she went, plunging her magic spade deep into the Earth, creating craters that spewed out molten fire. Some places were too shallow for her fire; others were too near the sea and were flooded with salt water when the tide came in.

On Kauai, the northernmost tip of the islands, Pele found an ideal place and claimed the spot as her own. But Namakaokahai, who secretly had followed her family to Hawaii, was hiding in the clouds, overseeing their actions. Upon witnessing smoke rising from a newly formed mountain, Namakaokahai rushed down and pounced on the fire spirit. They engaged in brutal combat, both vowing to be the sole survivor. When the battle was over, it was Pele who was left for dead, her life force drained from her limp body. Being an indomitable sorcerer, however, Pele ran her last vestige of life force through her body and charged the energy circuit. Renewed by precious mana, Pele rose up and again set out to accomplish her mission.

On Maui Pele discovered that the crater Haleakala provided an unlimited supply of magma for her hearth. While she set up house, her family waited nearby, ready to provide assistance if Namakaokahai attacked again. From her lookout station in the sky, where she was ever on the watch, the sea goddess noticed a disturbance on Maui. As the smoke became more and more voluminous and the sky grew darker, she realized that Pele was indeed alive and well, and had taken up residence at Haleakala. Biding her time while her desire for vengeance grew, Namakaokahai finally descended to the mountain in a surprise attack.

Pele had only to cry out for her small army to defend her against the goddess of the sea, but she did not. Pele was inflated with seismic power and felt certain that this time she could win the battle alone. On the western slope of the crater the fire spirit and the water goddess engaged in a long and fierce combat. Although they both had extraordinary resources and powers, Namakaokahai tore Pele apart, limb from limb, tossing her lava bones across the seashore. The other members of the family were devastated by Pele's death and grieved at her loss. However, Namakaokahai, the heinous one, celebrated the annihilation of her competitor.

After Pele's death, the goddess of the sea continued to patrol the territory she conquered, and daily looked out over the Pacific, scanning the lands for any invaders. One day, as her gaze moved across the island chain, she noticed something unusual occurring on the Big Island. It didn't seem believable at first, but as she focused her vision she knew for certain that Pele lived. Volcanic smoke and fire were pouring out of Mauna Loa. As she studied the phenomenon longer, Namakaokakai was shocked to see a beautiful feminine form rising out of the volcanic ashes. Stunned, Namakaokahai realized her inability to destroy the resurrected, now immortal, spirit of Pele. Released from her mortal shell on the Big Island,

Origins

Pele had become an unconquerable deity, one of the pantheon of Hawaiian gods.

The story of Pele's mythic journey and search for her true home is, on one level, a metaphoric explanation of the geological creation of the Hawaiian island chain and the sometimes violent interaction of the natural forces that this involved. Interpreted from an esoteric perspective, it can be considered analogous to the individual's spiritual quest for enlightenment. In the classic tale the voyager plunges into a series of life experiences, searching for a place, a transforming moment that will trigger an awakening of his or her higher self, the true place of origins and personal power. The hero encounters many obstacles and defeats in the mythic journey, for it involves opposition not only by outside forces, but also by inner polarities that erupt into turbulent warfare in the quest for the Self. Usually, after a long search and many tests of the person's fortitude in the spiritual evolutionary process, the polarities become reconciled, as the *kundalini*, the life force, clears the blocks in the psycho-physical energy centers of the body. During the resurrection and transmutation of the quester, the *kundalini* mounts to the summit of the head and opens the portholes to the higher kingdoms. In that place the seeker finds primordial awareness and a home in the awakened self.

Within each of us is an inner mythology, which, perhaps, we inherit from self-work in progress from past lives. We create a persona by our conscious decisions and acts. In time, the inner mythology and the outer form become mirror images.

As we follow the inner directives we are led, step by step, from the labyrinth into spaciousness and clarity. For each of us who lives the shamanic paradigm, giving life to the vision and metaphor, the Spirit is visible in the present moment and empowers us through each consecrated action. The inner and outer events mark the way of transformation. A mythic journey is, after all, about discovering initiation.

In Hawaii, on the slopes of Kilauea, I came to experience the volcano as a manifestation and symbol of transformative power. To Pele, the volcano goddess, I turned in muse to understand the psychic volcanic components of my unconscious. By following metaphors and acting out my mythology as it unfolded within me, intuitive experiences led to many moments of realization and new levels of empowerment.

Living in Hilo, thirty miles from Kilauea, I frequently received images of smoke coming out of a cinder cone that was filled with glowing red magma. Before sleep, with my eyes closed, I saw a woman in a long fuchsia dress fly over the hot pool, her form lit by the incandescent fire beneath her.

During my menstrual time, as I bled, I thought of magma flowing out of the Earth. During a full moon I wondered if my volatile sister was longing for Lohiau, her lost lover, as I longed for a man on the other side of the world. When I drove out to a new lava flow and saw the red-hot trails of molten lava spilling down the sides of the mountain and over the roads, I experienced a sympathetic response in my female psyche and an enhanced sense of the esoteric powers within my body.

In the folklore and religions of many cultures fire is both a metaphor for, and a manifestation of, divinity and transformation. In Vedic religion, Agni, the fire god, is the intermediary between the human and the divine. He is the tongue of god upon which offerings are placed, and as the sacred fire is the microcosmic manifestation of the Absolute.

According to Hawaiian legend, fire is an emanation of the goddess Pele, who is both creator and destroyer of the island. Hawaii was born and continues to grow in size as a result of volcanic activity; at the same time, the lush crops raised on the rich volcanic soil are incinerated by the molten lava fields.

On the Big Island there are many who believe that Pele resides within Halemaumau, the crater of Kilauea, and claim to have seen her feminine form amidst the smoke of the spewing volcano. Mary Kuwena Pukui, anthropologist and scholar of Hawaiian studies, witnessed the goddess in her spirit form. As a child, along with friends and relatives, she observed a ball of fire moving slowly down from the Kilauea crater, which then rolled up the side of the enormous Mauna Loa, Pele's second home.[*]

There are many who pay homage to the fire goddess, and traces

---

[*] Joe Mullins, *The Goddess Pele*, Honolulu, Tongg Publishing Co., 1977, p. 32.

Origins

of their devotion can be found. While hiking in the Ka'u desert, with its long stretches of desolate black lava fields, my son found a packet of dried taro leaves wrapped around dollar bills, and a bottle of massage oil – someone's private offering. 'That belongs to Pele – return it quickly,' I said. Josh immediately arranged the items on the dried magma just as he had found them. Even as I honored the devotion of another, I was also concerned about stirring up the ire of the goddess.

Formalized ritual still takes place at the crater of Kilauea. The *kahuna* – priests and priestesses of the ancient Hawaiian religion, Huna – who attend Pele, present their offerings to her sacrificial fire, asking her to spare people's lives and homes. It is claimed that when Pele is satisfied with their attentiveness, her mood changes from wrathful to gracious.

As in Hawaii and India, the South Sea Islanders have their fire deity to whom they have made their offerings. She is the goddess from whom all sources of fire originated. In Micronesia and Polynesia there is a story in which the boy Maui tries to steal the magical fire which resides in the head of their goddess. Her head contains the master fire which gives her powers and burns to a lesser degree in other body parts.

The metaphor of fire as the source of spiritual and supernatural power also has its correspondence within the yogic systems of India and Tibet, as an esoteric fire flowing through the body of adepts practising certain prescribed tantric disciplines. Even as the volcanoes in Hawaii are situated on the royal line of the Ring of Fire, so in the human body the etheric source of fire runs along the course of the spine through conduits and energy centers. As the inner fire, or *kundalini*, reaches the crown of the head, a psycho-physical transformation occurs in the initiate. Filled with the light of the sacred fire, the adept sacrifices old fixed patterns and habits. Tremendous disruption in the energy system can occur if inner conflicts, blocks and negativity are not worked with psychologically and with spiritual guidance before or concurrent with raising the energy. People traveling the paths of the shaman and self-realization work with this great energy system, along with the forces of light and dark, until they reach resolution and clarity.

So it is with a volcano. As a living being, the mountain fills itself

Volcanic Visions

with primordial fire and blows out obstacles through the cone. Kilauea can be viewed as a microcosmic house for the Earth's *kundalini*, while Pele can be understood metaphorically as the Goddess Kundalini, goddess of fire and transformation.

Characteristic of the shamanic archetype, Pele dwells in the depths of the Earth. In her volcanic domain she uncovers the mysteries of the Earth, which are synonymous with the mysteries of her being. In visionary flight she travels up into the ethers in a firework, then plunges down into the fiery depths, the womb of herself.

Looked at cross-culturally, these shamanic attributes are similar to those of the Greek goddess Persephone. Given a pre-patriarchal interpretation,* Persephone descends into the underworld on a shamanic journey into the interior of herself for six months of the year. With her descent, the visible vegetation becomes dormant and appears to die. When she emerges to ordinary consciousness in the spring, she retains the vision and enhanced powers achieved while meditating deep in the recesses of her mind and transforms the outer world by quickening the seeds and birthing process.

In a patriarchal interpretation of the mythology Persephone is the oppressed queen in the shackles of her husband–master, Pluto, her polar opposite in nature. She is the embodiment of birth and renewal, while he personifies raw power and destruction: they are integral to each other in the cycle of birth, death and rebirth. Post-patriarchally, viewed as symbolic positive and negative, female and male facets of the psyche, Persephone and Pluto represent archetypal psychological components that when polarized are destructive, but when harmonized lead to transformation. Thus inner freedom and rebirth in the psyche evolve only with the eventual reconciliation of these two inner forces.

Similarly, in Hawaiian folklore Pele is portrayed as the embodiment of both creation and destruction. As a quintessential goddess, she integrates these positive and negative forces and is sustained by the mana, or life force, within her.

The myths of the underworld are, perhaps, part of the collective

---

*Charlene Spretnak, *Lost Goddesses of Early Greece: A Collection of Pre-Hellenic Mythology*, Boston, Beacon Press, 1981, p. 106.

unconscious. In the *Tibetan Book of the Dead* the guardians of the underworld are fearful specters until recognized as aspects of the mind. Their negativity is dissolved when we realize that the true nature of the mind is luminous and without form. The archetypes that appear when we are living and while we are making passage into the next world are aspects of our own minds that need to be transformed by compassionate awareness. When transformed, the archetypes become allies and guardians leading us to a higher plane of existence, whether in this world, or the next.

When I was a child of four I had a dream of a king with long silver hair riding towards me on a black horse. As he came close, I noticed he looked much like my father, who was then in his fifties and graying. The king invited me to see his kingdom inside a cave, and I eagerly agreed, for the adventure and to see the wondrous things he told me about. The king sat me in front of him and together we rode until we came to the cave. It was coffin-black inside and the air was stagnant. Eventually, however, my eyes adjusted to the darkness, and beautiful, jeweled artifacts became visible along the walls. I was thrilled by the shimmering colors and wanted to touch each jewel.

As I got off the horse, the king and horse vanished, leaving me alone in the cave. The desire to explore was replaced by an overwhelming fear. There seemed to be little oxygen in the cave – I was barely breathing, but ran in panic, trying to find an exit. I awoke in a sweat, suffocating under the covers.

Several years ago I had an astrology reading in which I was told that my chart reveals that I am living a Persephone–Pluto myth. The astrologer, Tony Joseph, encouraged me to consciously learn the mysteries of these archetypes, so that I could master their lessons instead of being victimized by the negative aspect of their energies. He said that my path is that of the shaman, and that I must learn to walk the razor's edge between light and dark, between the underworld and the higher worlds. The shaman's domain is the interior realm of the archetypes, where Persephone is one of the guardians.

The dream I had at the age of four came directly from the unconscious, long before I had knowledge of the Persephone–Pluto myth. The meeting of the archetypes in the dream gave me a script to work from that has been relevant throughout my life. After interviewing contemporary women shamans and publishing *Shape Shifters*, it became important for me to go on a vision quest and explore my inner mythology.

When I was seven years old, my teacher read us a story about a boy named Pablo, who lived in Mexico. One day Pablo saw magma break out of his father's cornfield. He watched it grow into a hill, and then a mountain. He watched it grow into a violent mountain, terrorizing the people, but also filling them with awe and veneration. Like the coming of the Lord on Mount Sinai, when as a burning bush a righteous and vengeant God spoke to Moses, Mount Paricutin roared and threw thunderbolts of liquid fire. Pablo and his priest got down on their knees and prayed to Jesus Christ, the most powerful son of God.

Goose-flesh and bubbles mingled in the bath that night while I recounted the story of Pablo to my mom. I was electrified by the thought of the volcano growing in his field. There in the tub I declared my intention to see an active volcano in this lifetime.

In 1987 Kilauea was erupting. I flew to Hawaii with Josh, my ten-year-old son, to make the volcanic island our home.

2

THE CALLING

Kilauea

Maybe it's the coconut milk
maybe it's the foamy surf
maybe it's the lava slowly flowing down the mountain
or the scent of sweet plumeria blossoms . . .
or maybe it's something about to erupt in me

During the six-hour flight from the mainland I was straining forward in my seat until we landed in Honolulu. On leaving the plane I immediately experienced the soft, damp atmosphere, and smelled the ginger, plumeria and pikake flowers being sold on flower carts outside the airport. A warm rain hit my face for a few seconds, then passed by. I shook out my hair, took a deep breath of the intoxicating air and felt my hips swaying in response to the rhythm of the atmosphere. There was a tremble of anticipation in my belly. Josh's eyes were bright with excitement and a fine line of perspiration touched the curls on his forehead.

The first thing we discovered was that our luggage had not been transferred to our inter-island flight, so we grabbed it and dragged it from one terminal to the next at a frantic pace, to catch our soon-to-be-departing plane. Airborne again, we both stared down at the ground, trying to see every detail, as though we had entered a magic kingdom. Below we saw the volcanic range, and the long coastline lit up in the dusky Hawaiian sunset. Finally, we sat back, and after an hour of silent anticipation, the plane circled above a dark island.

We had visited the island two years earlier, and I was so entranced by the experience that I had returned there in dream and imagination many times. But now the darkness below looked formidable. We were landing, the two of us, mother and child, in a Pacific culture we knew only as tourists and where we knew no one.

When we left the plane and had retrieved our luggage, there were no more car rentals available, so I ordered a cab. The woman driver took an immediate liking to Josh, so she had a lot to say. I asked her about the weather over the last few days, whether it had been very hot or humid.

'No – but it has been very voggy. Pele, she has been acting up and the sky is all hazy from her fumes. People in Kalapana are worried that they will lose their homes because Pele is mad. The *ha'oles** built a geothermal plant and are tapping into her. She doesn't like that . . . And now the rangers at the Volcanic Park are charging admission to get into our sacred site. Pele is going to get back. She will blow the whole damn park up. She likes to show off her beauty and have people come see her. She doesn't hurt anybody. But now they charge admission for her home, she gets mad. The island belongs to us Hawaiians. The park is part of our sacred land. If we Hawaiians have to pay to honor her, Pele will blow the whole thing up.'

I listened intently, and at the same time strained to see out in the dark. I thought maybe I could get a glimpse of the erupting volcano against the sky.

'Oh, you can't see from here,' she said. 'Kilauea is thirty miles away. Although two years ago, you could. She was fountaining then, so pretty, lighting up the night. Now you have to drive around through Kalapana, where you can see a red glow coming from the new vent.'

The taxi driver dropped us off at the University Family Housing apartments. I had sold our furniture and car to make the move, so we were glad to see that our new home was partially furnished. As we pulled in our heavy luggage and dropped it on the floor, my son and I stared at each other and then out the window into the dark. 'I sure hope this was a good idea,' he said.

I looked out through the screen door at the outline of a slightly swaying palm and breathed in the faint scent of ginger blossoms. I shivered and said, 'I do too . . .'

---

* *Ha'ole* translates roughly as 'foreigner', 'outsider', 'white person'.

The Calling

It didn't take long for my son to make friends at the local school. Luckily for him, he has brown skin. One of the neighbor kids, who was blue-eyed and blond, fresh from Oregon, found it hard being called *ha'ole* by the other kids. After his first day at school Josh came home and told me about meeting a kid in class. The boy said to him, 'Brah, wha' island you from?' Josh answered, 'I'm not from an island.' The boy retorted, 'Wha', you born on a *ship*?'

I spent the first couple of weeks orienting myself on the island. Psychically, I dowsed my way around, sensing the hot spots or geological places that most magnetized me. I also put the radar on to connect to those people who were somehow linked to my quest and to my calling to the island. At a health food store in Hilo I saw an old lover who is now a Buddhist monk. It had been fifteen years since we had seen each other. The attraction was still there, but we also felt a shyness because of the time that had elapsed and the changes in our lives.

Ananda, Josh and I went to a little café on Ponahawaii Street. There was good humor and chemistry between us all. Ananda, youthful, with shaved head, full of laughs and love, bonded well with my son over jokes and sodas. In the days that followed he became a bridge between my past and present life.

But the deepest level of experience in the first few weeks took place at night. As I lay on the bed, aware of the faint scent of plumeria blossoms, listening to the rustle of palms, I thought of a man who lives on the other side of the world. While I slept near the foot of a volcanic mountain, he was deep in meditation at the foot of the Himalayas. I could hear his bell and conch shell in my dreams. It was taboo for us to be lovers physically, but in moments of quiet he appeared to me as an essence. Maybe it was the intoxication of the air and the beauty of the night that induced the phantom, but it was in the dream state that he appeared most clearly in astral visions.

> Each night the vision more vivid
> the call more deep
> I awaken, my heart pounding
> his breath a part of mine.

Volcanic Visions

I awaken to my desire
and recognize his visitation.

He doesn't know where I live
and yet he finds me.
I don't respond with letter
or word and yet he reads
the resonance of my heart
as I open the doors
of my dream.

By day I began to focus on the experience of living near an active volcano. I listened to the news reports of the progress of Pele's flow. Frequently there was a new vent threatening individual homes or communities. I wrote down details of the latest detours, information I'd need while exploring the active sites. Reading about the history of the volcanoes of Hawaii and the folklore of Pele made the mythic dimension seem all the more real. In my room I created a small shrine, on which I placed offerings of fresh fruits and flowers in a gesture of friendship to the spirit monarch of the land.

One evening, accompanied by Josh and his friends Mike and Pete, I drove the thirty miles to the Volcanic National Park, with the intention of seeing the fire of the lava trails, which would be more visible in the dark. As we reached the volcanic heartland we were impressed by the miles of old lava flows on both sides of the road. In some areas heavy fog rolled in, and, with only the car's headlights to break up the impenetrable blackness, I drove slowly through the eerie thick of it. After about twenty minutes, the kids were giggling nervously. They entertained each other with ghost stories until Pete yelled for them to stop. We were all unnerved by the profound darkness.

It was cold in the park, but we rolled down the car windows so that I had greater visibility. After about an hour I suddenly became aware of a drastic change in the air quality: we were inside a thick pocket of volcanic fumes. The boys coughed from the stench of sulfur, and I began struggling to breathe. 'Roll up the windows quick!' Josh yelled. I was frightened, yet I wasn't ready to turn around immediately and drive back through miles of almost zero

The Calling

visibility. The red glow on the horizon looked close at hand, so I drove forward tentatively, hoping and praying that the air would clear. To our intense relief, it did.

After a long drive, and with the mounting tension, my imagination began to expand. The boys had been silent for a long time. Partly to break the silence and partly to entertain myself, I asked them, 'Doesn't this seem like a perfect place to see a UFO? It's totally deserted out here.' Silence. 'Has anyone heard of any sightings on the island?' My son's friends shook their heads. Since they were already on edge, it probably wasn't a good time to ask.

Finally, we came to a barricade on the road and empty cars lined up in a long row on either side of the highway. Beyond the barricade there were flashes of light and distant voices. We got out of the car, shivering in the darkness, mainly from anticipation. Ahead of us I saw a path off the side of the highway. I called out, 'This way, guys.' We walked in silence. None of us knew what we were going to see and there was an element of fear in trusting ourselves to the whims of the goddess Pele. I stopped at a sign that I could just make out in the darkness. It said, 'Hazardous Area for People with Respiratory Problems'. We had already breathed what I hoped was the worst of the gas and I didn't want to give up at this point, so I hurried ahead and joined the boys in picking our way over the cooled lava. What we saw first was what seemed to be a long stretch of bonfires. Streams of flickering lights flowed down the mountainside, descending to the area near where we were standing.

Close by, at the edge of the burning lava field, was a group of about a dozen people. After a few minutes a ranger joined us and stood next to me. In answer to my questions about the safety of standing so close to an active flow, she told me that the eruptions from Kilauea are relatively safe, as the nature of the Hawaiian volcanoes is to release slow, non-violent flows. The park geologists keep tabs on the active volcanoes and are able to predict if there will be any activity that will pose a threat to people.

As we watched the live, slowly moving magma, I asked the ranger if she had ever seen any unusual or unaccounted for phenomena while in the park. 'There have been reports of fireballs,' she said, 'and other things.'

'Many people on the island still believe in Pele,' I commented. 'Do you?'

She nodded.

Staring out at the spectacle created by Earth magic, one moment I felt elated at being witness to the genesis of the Earth at the will of the Mother Goddess; the next, I felt a nihilistic pang, with the realization that my human existence is just another lava flow. The emptiness, the non-attachment of reality became clear. A Buddhist chant began revolving in my mind: 'There is no other than emptiness ... emptiness is no other than form ... form is no other than emptiness ... emptiness is no other than form ... gone ... gone beyond ... the goer goes ...' For a long while I suspended thought and stared into the flickering light of volcanic fire.

Then, as if by some command to return, the boys' voices filtered back in. 'This is rad! Really rad! I wish I could take some pictures back to the mainland ...' They were giddy all the way home, singing a raucous round of 'Bottles of Beer on the Wall'. Laughing until they had tears in their eyes, they were high from the volcanic fumes, from an imagined peril they had survived and from the sensational beauty and drama they had just witnessed and, in some way, been part of. I was as pensive as they were rowdy. The drive through the darkness was easier the second time round, with no gas clouds. Venus was bright in the black sky and I was haunted by the eerie beauty of the starlit lavascape.

A few days after our trip to Kilauea I was shocked to read in the *Hilo Tribune* that a woman from Hayward, California had died from an asthmatic attack brought on by volcanic fumes she inhaled while leaning over a sulfur vent in the park. The gas pocket still fresh in my mind, I said to myself, 'There by the grace of the goddess went the boys, and I.'

The fear of danger, however, did not keep me away. I had come to the island to learn the mysteries and lore of the volcano and the goddess Pele, so now I drove to the coastal town of Kalapana, which legend claims will be taken back and swallowed up by Pele, to see an eruption. The area is imbued with powerful magnetic energy. Old hippies live in the coconut groves that go down to the sea even though hazard signs warn of danger from falling coconuts. Fear of being knocked out by a coconut is no

The Calling

deterrent. Empty husks are strewn across the shore in the morning, with machete-cut holes across the tops. Traces of breakfast in bed.

Public vehicles were not allowed on the road because of the eruption, so I parked my car along the side of the beach and walked a couple of miles in to see a fresh lava flow. On the way I passed cars and road signs buried beneath a recent flow. One sign caught my attention, the words still visible above the lava: 'Volcano Reality – A Piece of Paradise – Cheap!' I laughed and was glad that Pele showed them who is realtor and who is tenant.

At the end of the road I came to a sign saying 'Go No Further'. Behind it was a narrow fence, acting as a barrier to the steaming flow. A ranger sitting in his car saw me approaching and eagerly got out to meet me, tired of being the lone sentinel guarding the encroaching lava. I introduced myself and we exchanged brief bios. When I told him I wanted to have a closer look, Ranger Roger helped me over the fence, allowing me to stand within a few inches of the live magma. He jumped atop a recently cooled hunk and stared at the sky and the mountain facing us while I examined the rough, ropy surface of the *pahoehoe* lava, and the bubbling viscous *aa* lava, which comprised most of the huge mass.

Roger, who looked firmly planted on the rock, now warmed to tell me an island story about a group of vacationers who had visited the island a few years before. They had brought a picnic lunch with them to enjoy while viewing the fantastic scenery and breathing in the fresh volcanic air. Unfortunately for them, however, an earthquake ripped through the park and the ground opened up, swallowing picnickers and table. There haven't been many other recent reported deaths related to the volcano, Roger tried to assure me. I wondered if he had read about the woman from Hayward.

Just as I was adding the idea that the ground might open up at any moment to my list of perils of living on a volcanic island, I was distracted by the sight of four men behind Roger. Like an apparition, they walked slowly over the top of the fresh lava, dressed from head to toe in what appeared to be astronaut suits. As they slowly made their way towards us in silence my first thought was that they were astronauts in training, preparing themselves for live lava flows on other planets. An even more entertaining thought was that they were alien astronauts acclimating themselves on terrestrial lava.

Volcanic Visions

Roger seemed familiar with them and accepted their appearance nonchalantly. As one of the men came close to where I stood, I asked him who they were. 'Volcanologists,' he said abruptly. Mechanically, the 'firewalkers' continued their progress to the edge of the lava, jumped over the fence, one by one, and proceeded to their car, parked at the side of the molten field. One of the men tipped his hand to us before driving away into the lavascape.

After their departure, I looked at the ranger standing on his rock and at myself standing within inches of the bubbling lava. I scanned the black silhouette of Kilauea and the moonlike wasteland stretching in all directions, meeting the azure sky. We were standing on a razor's edge, a thin cusp between inner and outer space, where primeval and mythic merge.

3

THE VOG

There is a danger wind on the alert tonight
blowing the palms and causing chaos on the mountain roads.
My passion is on a rampage as I search the dark for my heart
in a night of shaking trees.

The smell of burning was so strong it permeated my clothes and hair. I awakened to the suffocating smell of sulfur. Afraid to breathe, the stench of burning put me on the alert like an animal in the forest preparing to flee from fire. Having been told that the volcano is predictable, that Pele would not take Hilo, my fear was controlled. Below the rationalizations, however, the specters of fear danced around me. I tried to lull myself to sleep in the arms of the guardian who whispers in my dreams, on a night when the curtains were blown back and forth by a cool and smoky wind.

In the morning the curtains remained shut and I entered in my journal, 'Hilo has been under a curse for three weeks. Swallowed by a low thick haze, worse than any smog I've experienced in L.A. The cloying air makes breathing difficult, the stinging pain behind the eyes intolerable. Cut off from activity except for visits to the doctor's office, where town's people have similar complaints.'

'Pele is killing me,' one man said to the receptionist. 'My nose, my eyes burn like wild fire. If the damned *ha'oles* would leave her alone, we wouldn't have no problem. But no can do. They come here and stir up trouble.' The receptionist agreed while writing down his complaints.

I heard confirmed, as I had many times, that on the island Pele is at the heart of reality, a sentient being with anthropomorphic passions. If we violated her sanctuary, she filled our days and nights with poison. When her domain was respected, she offered us mangoes grown from her belly and coconuts suckled from her breast.

Volcanic Visions

After seeing the doctor I went back to bed, staring at the four walls, questioning why I felt called to the island. Lying there submerged in torpor, the hours weighed down by oppressive vog, I slept through the smoke-brown day and evening until 1 a.m., when I wakened to a death-like gas enveloping me. In terror I imagined red-hot lava surrounding our apartment.

I had read too many graphic details about the 36,000 people who had died in 1883 – in the explosion 'heard around the world' – when Krakatoa erupted and enveloped them in darkness, sucking up their breath and peeling off their flesh. Centuries earlier, an entire continent had been buried beneath the sea as the ash issued from the jaws of Thera. In recent years I had read about the people who had refused to leave Mt St Helens while it rumbled: the 20,000 who said their prayers in Bogotá, Colombia, months before being swallowed by a volcanic mud slide, and the 1,600 in Cameroon who were suffocated by the volcano's toxic fumes.

The people who died had depended on the volcano for inspiration, for lush crops, for mythology – and were swallowed by their deity. I, too, summoned by the volcano, had fallen under her spell. I believed that Pele, ally and sister, would awaken the slumbering power within me, freeing me from the bonds of exploitation, self-doubt and invalidation delivered by patriarchal minds. But now, in the dark, all dreams shut off, I lay in waking nightmare choking on sulfur and mercury, the fourth round of bronchitis, the fourth round of antibiotics, the fourth round of volcanic fumes draining away my life force.

To use toxins to awaken, instead of sink into a permanent sleep, the alchemist transmutes the poison into nectar, the dross into gold.

> Breathe in ignorance, and breathe out wisdom.
> Breathe in lust, and breathe out clear light.
> Breathe in hatred, and breathe out love.

So says the Buddhist metaphysician.

By dawn fear had dissipated. Blue pierced the haze. Pulling up the shades, I let the sky in and read the morning's headline: 'Pele Takes Queen's Bath.' A historical landmark gone in a moment. The warm, tropical pool had been used by the Hawaiian royal family

The Vog

and enjoyed by generations of islanders. Now the true monarch of the land reclaimed the pool, filling it with magma.

Reading on, a feature article in the newspaper provided valuable tips on ways to cope with volcanic haze. A list of suggestions compiled by the Hawaiian chapter of the American Lung Association provided practical, common-sense tips: 'If possible, stay inside, close windows and doors when smoke or haze is heavy. Drink plenty of fluids to help you cough and loosen mucus. Relax, take it easy that day; don't exert yourself.' A couple of suggestions, however, were not particularly helpful, such as, 'Anticipate more trouble if you've had a cold or bronchitis within the last six weeks.' And the one I thought almost useless was, 'Because the sulfur gases emitted by the volcano are water soluble, it will probably be helpful to wear two surgical masks at a time and dampen the outside one. This will absorb some of these gases as well as particles, but if you find it difficult to breathe, don't use it.'[*] I knew from experience, however, that the tips put out by the advisory body were more than a bit of whimsy. They contained important instructions for survival on a volcanic island.

The vog was now blowing Kona-side. By noon the pall had been swept away, the sky was magnetic blue, and yesterday's afflicted side of the island had shifted from a hellish plane to a heavenly one. I drove into town to do errands and exchanged smiles with people on the streets, mutually reassured that we were in paradise. Driving home, I noticed birds singing loudly in the palms and fruit trees. Ferns seemed larger, swollen with humidity, stretching their fronds to the sun.

The doctor had told me to rest a few more days, but I was breathing more easily and felt a desire to see the awesome beauty of Halemaumau, the two-mile crater of Kilauea. I had been there before with friends, but this time I would go there alone.

I drove the thirty miles absorbed in thought. Arriving at the parking lot near the crater, half an hour later, I went over to the edge of the chasm and looked down into the earth's womb, the 'house of everlasting fire'. Vapors rose up in streams from the

---

[*] 'Tips on Handling Volcanic Haze Told', *Hilo Tribune Herald*, April 1, 1987.

Volcanic Visions

titanic opening that looked bottomless. Suddenly I was gripped by horror, by the devastating power of the divinity who lives within the volcano. Into the depths of Halemaumau I stared, remembering the primordial womb of the creator, the darkness from which I was born. Maybe it was because I was alone, that I had no buffer from the fears and specters lurking in my unconscious. I had no one there to laugh away the open-ended terrain of my imagination.

I forced myself to stare into the gigantic black void. This, too, was Pele — a potentially awesome power that could not be controlled. She was there, a breathing, panting spirit. I stood on the edge of the volcano, facing the goddess on her own turf. I looked into the smoking house of Pele, and waited as the prophets of Atlantis had waited, feeling Thera stamping her feet, smoke ascending from her nostrils. When Thera exploded 3,600 years ago, the Minoan culture sank into the Aegean Sea. When Pele erupted 12,000 years ago, Lemuria drowned in the Pacific.

From which vent did Pele emerge as a roaring, cataclysmic giant? From which hole did she reach out with fiery blasts, pulling everything down into her seething cauldron? Like a moth to a flame, I stared into the chasm, into the face of the Goddess — the creator and destroyer who rises from her own ashes, who had unleashed an explosion of macrocosmic proportion, giving birth to the universe fifteen billion years ago. As a microcosmic deity within each person, the Goddess Kundalini also waits, coiled at the seat of the spine, until she rises up the caldera of the head and explodes, giving birth to volcanic vision.

Staring into the abyss of the volcano had been like staring into the face of my own death and the fears surrounding it. Afterwards, I wanted to retreat for a while within the boundaries of Hilo, my world. At home, in my writing and in literature I found a safe haven from which to converse with the primordial forces. That night I took out the *Tibetan Book of the Dead* and read through the vivid descriptions of the guardians of the underworld, the spirits who evoke terror in the uninitiated, but become initiators and guides to transformation and liberation in those who have gone through the necessary esoteric training.

There occurs for each person in some lifetime, the desire to pierce the veil of obscurity surrounding mystical lore. By seeing into the symbolic world a coded representation of his or her psychological make-up, the quest for transforming the inner reality becomes mirrored on the stage of conscious life. The protagonist learns to integrate on the outer stage the inner forces of dark and light.

Putting down the book, I opened my window to let in the trade wind. The air was infused with the scent of ocean and plumeria, and my eros awakened after long, suffocating nights. In a vase on my shrine the orchids looked moist and alive, pastel and etheric, contrasting with the hibiscus blazing crimson and bold. As a kind of prayer I wrote a few lines to allay the longing and the restless beauty of the evening.

> I look into the orchid
> and see a shimmering
> across the miles
> of heat rising more intensely
> than from the fresh lava
> flowing in Kalapana.
> Past the dripping flow,
> across the smoking mountain top,
> across three oceans,
> I see a man contemplating a flower
> opening his hand to me.

4

PELE MYSTERIES

Pele, the shape shifter, lay down on a lava bed of her creation and surrounded herself in a gossamer veil of sleep. Her astral body was waiting for her as she entered lightly into the dream state. Hi'iaka, spirit of the dance, stood by, guarding Pele's body while she took off in flight. The empty shell of the fire goddess appeared like that of an old crone – the third face of Pele. In her first two phases she appears alternately as the young maiden, an enchanting seductress, and as a mother with the power of life and death, the great goddess who gives birth. In her third phase she is the reaper, bringing death to old forms, transforming them into something new. The triune faces of the goddess – maiden, mother, crone – are the three faces of woman and her mysteries.

It was in her maiden shape that Pele projected herself into the astral world in search of a lover and husband. Hi'iaka took seriously the responsibility of guarding Pele's body. She knew her sister loved her dearly, but was also given to fits of anger when crossed, which could lead to the volcanic destruction of Hi'iaka's favorite haunts in the rain forest or by the sea. While Hi'iaka stood by, Pele flew along an astral trail, responding to a dream beat that grew louder in her sleep. First she went to Hilo, then along the coast to Lapahoehoe. The hypnotic sound teased her by vanishing in the ether just as she approached the place from which she thought it emanated. The hula beat began to stir the trees and was caught up by the wind, drawing Pele across the shores to Maui. Again the phantom sound eluded her. Then it became very distinct and, with certainty of her path, Pele flew through the veil light until she arrived on the shores of Kauai. Slipping through the gossamer dream surrounding her, she emerged as a beautiful, voluptuous woman. The drum beat was close and her passions swelled as she responded to its call.

Pele wanted to be ready for her rendezvous. She went to the forest and gathered flowers for her hair, weaving red lehua blossoms

Pele Mysteries

into a garland for her neck, dressing in maile vines and ferns from the dwelling place of the gods. Pele walked along the beach, her hips swaying in time with the rustling palms, the hypnotic sound drawing her across the sand, a man's tender voice entwined with the drum beat. She followed her desire, arriving at last at Haena, a long house for dancing, decorated with exquisitely colored mats for a festival. It was the house of the young chief Lohi'au, who had brought together many visiting chiefs to engage in sports and an exchange of chants and hula drums.

Outside the house the villagers were having their own party. When Pele emerged from the forest dressed in flowers and leaves, the people stared at her as if she were an apparition, a goddess of a woman. The disguised deity made her way through a passage created by the throngs of people and entered the long house. Knowing well her place, without hesitation Pele seated herself on one of the soft royal mats. The gathered chiefs were astonished by her presence, and one asked her where she came from.

'From Kauai,' she said coyly.

The high chief Lohi'au looked into her sultry eyes and said, 'Tell me the truth. Where do you come from, woman who appears from nowhere?'

Seeing he would not accept her evasiveness, she said, 'I come from Puna, on Hawaii.'

'Ah,' he said. 'Then I welcome you to my house. It is known as the "tree of life". All I can offer is my hospitality and my home.'

Pele looked at Lohi'au and knew him to be the destination of her soul travel. 'I accept,' she said demurely.

They spent many days in 'the tree of life' as husband and wife, making love and singing the chants of the gods. Lohi'au made arrangements for another celebration in honor of their union. Three beautiful women arrived for the festival, whom Pele recognized as sorcerers, the guardians of the caves of Haena. They did not recognize her, however, for Pele's aura was swollen with love and fulfilment. There was no sign of the volatile spirit of the volcano goddess. The night of the feast, Kilinoe, the most beautiful of the sorcerers, made fragrant garlands and placed them enticingly around the neck of Lohi'au while secretly uttering love charms. Pele observed the wiles of Kilinoe and placed a counter-spell on

Volcanic Visions

Lohi'au so he would ignore the other woman's advances. Pele, fragrant with the perfumes of Puna, began to dance the hula and called upon the god Lono and his brothers, requesting each of them to release the soft, gentle winds to caress the faces of the guests. Then the volcano goddess called upon stronger winds to join her, which responded to the cadences and commands of her voice as rain pelted the long house of the chiefs.

Many of the people outside the long house became frightened and cried out when they saw the sea foaming and tossing wild waves to shore. The clouds brought foreboding of hurricane weather. As if to break the spell, Kilinoe of Haena said, 'She has created an illusion. The sound of the wind and the waves is only the sound of leaves in the trees and the din from the people talking together at once.' In response, Pele turned the winds back to their place of origin and allowed a peaceful energy to descend upon the gathering. Her voice became soft, bringing the magical weaving of words to an end.

Kilinoe, also known as a Moo or dragon woman, was full of spite at Pele's display of supernatural power. But she hid her rancor and politely requested that Pele exhibit the winds of Kauai, thinking them out of her domain. So the fire goddess began her chant to the local winds, calling first on the guardians of the mountains to bring the mists, then the flying gusts, until finally she summoned the howling forces that turn day into night. The sorcerers began to lose their self-assurance and became anxious about the powers of this extraordinary woman. As if to confirm their fears, Pele sang out about the deeds of the cave spirits and told all who could hear about how the dragon women unleashed evil winds to tear up the residents' homes and destroy the fruit trees in their island paradise. The chiefs listened closely to this song and were alerted to the evil intentions of the cave guardians of Haena. The three beautiful women, fearing that the chiefs, knowing their true nature, would attack them, rushed from the site back to the caves of Haena.

As if to fulfill the prophecy of the evil doings of the spirits of the caves, Pele unleashed the wind's catastrophic powers to assault the island, and brought her chant to a close. Members of the party fled. Chiefs and hula drummers vacated the place that had been a site of joyous gathering. Alone again in the long house, Lohi'au and Pele

Pele Mysteries

witnessed the thunder and lightning attacking the sky, the rain pelting down, cascading over the hillsides, while from afar they heard the roar of the ocean crashing on the sandy beach. Safe in the long house, they rested in the eye of the hurricane. As they lay together in his house, Lohiahu saw Pele in a new light: she was a prophet who had come to his land to foretell the evil that was unleashed that day.

The next morning, as the last howl died away, Pele turned over on the mat with her back to Lohi'au, straining to hear a voice that was calling her from far away. When she turned around to face the bronze chieftain, looking into his kahlua eyes, she wept and gripped his calloused hand, rough from beating the hula drum. He didn't understand her sudden grief: the storm had been fierce, but they had experienced only sweetness. After a long silence Pele said, 'I charged my sister to call me when it is time for my return to Puna.' He waited anxiously for explanation. Pele listened again to the faint strains of the chant that she had taught Hi'iaka. The incantation across the miles was a call to a wandering spirit to return home. 'The current is turning,' was all she said.

'You can't go,' he said. 'We are one.'

But Pele kissed him goodbye, tears streaming down her face, and said, 'I must respond to the call. But soon I will send my sister to bring you to me in Puna, where we will live in my home, "the house of everlasting fire".' On Lohi'au's mat Pele's form began to lose substance until there was only a sparkle of light and she was gone. As Pele departed into the veiled light she brought back a spirit of peace to the island, and left Lohi'au with a tranquil heart and the scent of lehua blossoms.

5

THE VISION

Veil light
oh veil light
comes with a hush
that beds the evening
and cloaks the thrush
who start off their journey
on a soft weathered flight
into the veil light
into the veil light.

I found parallels between the myths of the goddess and the mythic dimension in my life. The astral and dream states were familiar terrain in which I experienced a connection with 'the man from the other side of the world'. Because of those meetings, I came to know aspects of deity in each of us.

My activities on the volcanic island also became dreamlike, tinged with mythic themes. Josh and I met Ananda at the Buddhist temple for the Obon, the sacred community dance, at which he was one of the attending monks. When we arrived, he was in the shrine room offering prayers and flowers, and then shared with us the origins of the Obon.

During the time of the Shakyamuni Buddha, one of his students went into a deep meditation and saw his deceased mother in a hell realm – a hungry ghost world. The disciple was anguished to see his mother in this place, and implored Shakyamuni Buddha to help him to free her from hell. He was instructed: 'Feed the Buddha and the people.' After the disciple had followed this advice, he meditated again and saw to his joy that his mother had been freed from hell and now resided in heaven. The student jumped up with joy, and the other monks jumped up and rejoiced with him.

The Vision

The movements of the Obon dance thus symbolize the joy of the liberation of the deceased from the hell realm into the heavenly world through the prayers and merits offered by their loved ones.

Understanding more of the history, Josh and I joined with others in the sacred circle, following their graceful, ritualized movements. I prayed for my father and for my past love, who sometimes seems to hover so near from the other world. Within my mind I called on the deities to help him reach swift enlightenment. My son kept the content of his prayers quiet, in his own heart. Circling without a sound in the darkness, moving hands and feet in offering, we wove our thoughts into the circle many revolutions, until there was a feeling of completion. Then, silently, we slipped out of the mandala and paid our respects in the temple.

The next morning I awakened to a Hilo in full tropical bloom. Ananda called early and we made plans to spend the day together in the sun. After driving to Akaka Falls on the outskirts of town, we picnicked on a grassy knoll. It overlooked a foaming waterfall cascading over the 'boiling pots' below – the deep pits alongside the river where volcanic activity, which had long since ceased in this spot, had once heated the water.

It was a pleasure being with my 'new', old friend. Long ago he and I had lived together at the Buddhist Meditation Center in L.A. Together we had studied with a voice teacher, performed duets in public and shared many laughs and consciousness-expanding experiences. Ananda had wanted us to marry and record jazz vocals together, but I was young and not ready for commitment. I left L.A. for a different lifestyle up north while he turned his attention to a spiritual quest and became a monk. I delighted in our meeting again after so much transition. We had become different people in some ways, but shared old feelings of intimacy.

Sitting above the waterfall after we had exchanged life stories from when we had parted years ago, Ananda said that he often stopped at that spot to meditate before meeting a group of people at a hospice nearby. Although our plan had been to spend the day together in the sun, Ananda asked me to go to the hospice with him after lunch, and I agreed because he felt it was important that I experience that part of his life.

We drove a short distance through the outskirts of town and

pulled into the driveway of the old hospital wing. I was startled to hear yelps and cries, then saw that people had started for the car when they spotted Brother Ananda. Inside the community room a crowd assembled, waiting. A few people arrived in wheelchairs, while others sat down on chairs and sofas as well as they could with joints not functioning, their free movement curtailed. A man sat close to me on the couch and put his hand on my leg. It took me a few moments to adjust to having this stranger nestled near me. I had to work through my aversion to the smell, saliva and uninvited intimacy. My attention went out to those around me who needed to be nurtured, touched, related to.

Ananda led a song and many people put tremendous feeling into every word, dissolving boundaries within themselves. For a few suspended moments everyone let go of the pangs of pain. As we looked around at each other there was a connection in our human condition, all being vulnerable to suffering and karma.

Afterwards, Ananda gave a short closing talk, and said, 'Let's create good by being kind to each other. The good we create will come back to us.' I wondered how helpful it was to discuss karma with people in such deep physical and emotional pain. However many of the people in the room looked touched by his words, by his caring. He was offering his friends what was most precious for him to give, the teachings and inner presence that filled his life. His love was experienced as spiritual food. When we first arrived, I had thought about reproaching Ananda for not preparing me, but when we left I didn't want to mention it; by being unprepared, the experience had been that much deeper.

It was midday and there was a lot of sun yet, so we drove to a park in Hilo and strolled through the banyan trees imported from India and Sri Lanka. In silence we communicated the experience we had just shared and the beauty of our walk in the park. Ananda led us to a Japanese pavilion overlooking a pond filled with golden carp. We sat next to each other in the pagoda, close but not touching, our energies rippling back and forth as we watched the golden carp glide through the water.

As the weather turned sultry in Hilo, I began thinking more seriously about going out 'into the field' again to investigate the

The Vision

volcano I had come to the island to write about. With that intention, I drove to the town of Pahoa to get a full view of Kilauea's new cinder cone. At a roadside stand I bought a passion fruit shaved-ice cup. As I sat sucking the sweet syrup and fine crushed ice through a straw, I watched smoke ascending from the volcano about fifteen miles away. Absorbing the sun and the view, perspiration trickled down my neck, dampening my thin sarong, while my mind meandered from one thought to another. I thought about the swelling form in front of me, which grows daily, with each lava flow. I thought about how large the volcano could become, and how it has the power to rise up in cataclysmic upheaval – a revolution of revolutions. Old legends say that it has happened before, that a volcanic blast has thrown off the profane who believe that their destiny is to conquer the Earth.

Lingering for a while more and baking my skin in the sun, I brought out a newspaper from the car and propped it on the roadside picnic table. The one item I found of interest was an informal naming survey for Kilauea's new vent. It had been going on for a while and the choice had been narrowed down to three possibilities: Pu'u Ulumaki, meaning to continue to grow in fire; Na Kapa O Pele, the blanket of Pele; and Pu'u Kupaianaka, which translates as surprising, strange, wonderful, extraordinary. However, there was still an opportunity for readers to send in other suggestions, which, though not selected as contenders, the newspaper printed. Someone had suggested 'Naulu', which referred to Pele as the teaser, or being vexed by her teasing. A man in Kalapana suggested Pu'u O Nui Hewa, 'the hill that was a sinful mistake.' He was quoted as saying, 'The people made the mistake to remain silent [regarding the imposition of an entry fee to the Volcanic National Park], therefore the guilt lay with them. Pele herself would call [that] Pu'u O Nui Hewa. I belong to that mana, so I know . . .'[*] A woman named Minnie Kaawalua offered Halulu, which refers to the sound accompanying an eruption. She chose it because she heard the sounds of the volcano from where she lived. Each name reflected the giver's relationship to the volcano, and

---

[*] *Hilo Tribune Herald*, June 7, 1987.

varied according to whether the relationship was personal or academic, spiritually inspired or reflected a kinship between family or neighbors.

Although I could have sat longer and analyzed my own relationship to the volcano, I decided to drive directly to the newly erupting vent, despite the fact that it was late in the afternoon. As I neared Kilauea twilight surrounded the smoking cone. Town and society seemed eons away as I entered the primordial zone of the goddess. Her shadow blackened the sky with thick sulfuric vapors, which spread through the forest.

I circumnavigated the smoking mandala with my car and looked through the window at the red sparks flying over the rim of cinder cone. Surrounded by the pregnant forest spirit, I seemed to slip deeper and deeper into the shadows. Like an animal crouched in the darkness, I watched the glowing embers issue from the burning mountain, the primordial fires dripping down the sides. For a long time I lay in wait, watching, alone with the beginning of all things, alone with an erupting volcano.

There was nothing else to see, nothing else to do, but be in the presence of a burning mountain. I could understand why the old man of Mt St Helens refused to leave his cabin when the volcano was ready to blow. I could understand that his relationship to the mountain was so complete and total that there was nowhere else to run, nowhere to hide.

Something told me I must rouse myself, must pull away from the hypnotic vortex before I became sucked up by the burning forces of darkness. Slowly, I began to drive away from the magnetic power surrounding Kilauea, I tried to break through the time warp and my mesmerized state. After what seemed a very long time, I reached first Pahoa and then Kea'au, towns in which the vintage store fronts and homes are weatherbeaten and rustic enough for a movie set.

Leaving the towns, I came again to darkness, another stretch of road without city lights, retaining the impenetrableness of the volcanic island. What price to surrender to such magnetic presence? When dwelling in the mythic zones there is such a thin line ... I was deep in thought when I saw the fishing boats lit up in Hilo bay. As I neared home I realized I hadn't yet surfaced from the journey to Kilauea. Exhausted, and probably still in trance, I was glad Josh

The Vision

was spending the night at a friend's, as I felt too tired to make dinner or to communicate. With only enough energy to get a bite to eat, I fell into bed. My head felt heavy on the pillow and I sank into the twilight world, into a swirling fog, a residue of the volcanic terrain.

From out of the darkness brilliance suddenly burst through — dazzling lights silhouetted a space ship against the pitch blackness of a volcanic mountain. In the fleeting instance I felt a shock jolt through me. My body jerked forward in response to the electricity and, without thinking, I reached out my hand to touch the lights. Then, as if a switch had been turned off, the lights flickered and disappeared.

I sat up, fully awakened by the intensity of the apparition. The thought came to me that somehow information had been transmitted through my neuro-circuitry. I considered other possible explanations of the vision. The primordial landscape to which I had just journeyed had aroused my imagination, releasing archetypal images in my brain, projecting the image of the UFO. Although the explanation seemed more probable, it didn't alter my feeling of having been a recipient of transmission. The UFO image was an incongruity in relation to the events of the day.

Into the night I whispered 'Pu'u Kupaianaka', 'extraordinary', my name choice for the volcano. I fell asleep waiting for the next window opening on to the mythic zone.

6

GENESIS

*Mother
I
am
nourishing
the
world
and
growing
it
on
my
umbilical
cord
my
only
connection
to
life.*

After a long siege of vog, there followed a stretch of radiant days before the rain set in (contrary to an assumption by many first-time tourists, the rain in Hilo is cold). One such wet day in April I cozied up in a big cushioned chair in my living room and looked out the window at the rain splashing on the ferns and palms, the air shimmering with precipitation. I savored the feeling of being homebound, nowhere to go, the day to be filled with reading.

Looking through the newspaper, I saw a photo of Prince Philip on the cover of the island weekly. He was coming to Hawaii to be the chief dignitary at the dedication ceremony of the James Clerk Maxwell Telescope, housed atop Mauna Kea, the world's highest seamount. A *kahuna* priest would perform a spiritual blessing. I was intrigued by the event and the idea of these two men – one representing a sacred tradition of old Hawaii, the other a member of old European royalty – being brought together to christen this 'mirror of the universe'. An amazing instrument that has the capacity to view the origins of our universe by recording the level of heat released by the 'Big Bang' fifteen billion years ago. For me, living on the island, distant from the high-tech mainland, the event took on a mystique.

I called the University of Hilo Observatory and inquired about attending the ceremony. 'Certainly not,' said the man who answered the phone. 'I'm not even invited.'

Not deterred, I phoned the Mauna Kea Observatory and spoke to an astronomer, telling him I was a freelance journalist requiring a press pass for the event. He asked for whom I wrote, and I explained that I had a book being published by a British publisher, whose name he recognized.

'Agreed,' he said. He would contact the BBC when they arrived in two days and tell them I was to be included in their party. So it was all settled: he would run a security check, put my name on the list of invited media and arrange for me to ride up the mountain and lunch with the BBC.

Josh had laughed when, before making the calls, I had told him I was going to the mountain to see the prince. When I got off the phone, he was quiet.

Two days later I received a call from one of the coordinators of the event, who had just flown in from London. He told me I was invited to ride to Mauna Kea with his party and gave me instructions for meeting him the next day. On that rain-drenched morning of April 27, 1987 I jumped out of bed, dressed quickly and went to the designated press office on Komohana Street. After a brief introduction to the layout of the observatory and regulations concerning our dealings with the royal party, we collected our press packets, assembled in our respective vans and headed for the mountain.

The energy was elevated in our group. We enthusiastically exchanged information regarding our professional backgrounds and talked about the ways in which our personal world views influenced our work as investigative writers. They asked me philosophical questions concerning my motivation for writing *Shape Shifters*, and I asked them about their role as media in Britain and about their interactions with the royal family. There were vast differences in our approach to the event we were to cover. They were commissioned to report the concrete details of the dedication ceremony; I was a freelance writer looking for the hidden dimension, the mythological aspects of the ritual.

We shared a lot of laughs as well as reflective talk as we bounced along the unpaved Saddle Road to Mauna Kea, 'the white-capped mountain'. The patron deity of the mountain, Poli'ahu, the snow goddess, wears her mantle of snow on the highest crest most of the year, but she must have put it aside that morning: there was no snow in sight. We wound around the mountain base and saw cows grazing on the perennially grassy slopes. As we ascended, the vegetation disappeared, replaced by the craggy surface of the mountain, ragged from volcanic eruptions. During the last volcanic activity on Mauna Kea, estimated to have been around 4,500 years ago, there was a series of explosions that ripped open the sides of the mountain, leaving behind giant potholes.

I was reminded of the story about the battle that took place between Poli'ahu and Pele on these slopes. Both goddesses loved the ancient sport of *holua*-coasting, racing in long, narrow sleds down the grassy hillsides. One day Poli'ahu was exhibiting her prowess, whizzing down a hillside south of Hamakua. Pele, who prided herself as being the unrivalled champion of the sport, trembled with anger as she watched the *holua* champion from the snows. When the ground began to burn from Pele's rage, Poli'ahu knew the nature of her stunning rival. Pele threw off her disguise and called upon the seismic powers of Mauna Kea to break forth. From the underground chambers she beckoned the angry fires to come rushing out and burn down the slopes. Aghast, Poli'ahu raced up to the mountain top, where she seized the protective mantle she had put aside for the races. The lava had already singed her cloak, but she was able to reclaim it in time. Her power restored, Poli'ahu threw her precious mantle around the mountain and summoned the snow-bearing clouds to cool the seething lava that was pouring from the volcano at Pele's command. The magma cooled and hardened in the deep freeze called up by Poli'ahu. Although the ground still trembled and roared, Pele eventually was forced to retreat to the southern half of the island, withdrawing her magma forces back into the burning mountains of Kilauea and Mauna Loa. Mauna Kea continues to be the domicile of the exquisite, but some say cold-hearted, goddess of the snow.

'How ghastly!' said the woman sitting on my right, looking out at the pock-marked, barren landscape.

'Do you think so?' I asked wryly. 'Personally, I was slain by the primeval starkness of it. It's something like being on Mars, I've heard.'

'Yes! That's what I've heard,' said the man on my right, smiling.

The altitude became increasingly rarefied as we ascended the flanks of the old fire mountain, and the group was less communicative, staring out at the eerie volcanic lavascape in the rain. We stopped at Hale Pohaku, the halfway point to the mountain's summit, for a brief lunch and to acclimate before reaching the top. The building was a modern meeting hall, an anachronism in that primal world. I looked at the assembly of astronomers and media representatives – all men except for the two women in our party – swarming around the long tables spread with an assortment of buffet entrees. For the first time since initiating that adventure I felt shy.

From behind me someone put a hand on my arm. I turned around to find a tall, elegant, silvering man whose expression said, 'I understand the feeling.' But aloud he said, 'Let's eat. It will ward off altitude sickness, you know.' An astronomer, he was the representative for Canada, which had just joined Britain in sponsoring the infrared telescope at Mauna Kea. After enjoying our conversation over lunch, I rejoined the BBC group for the journey to the top.

As the van rounded the final windy bend we all exclaimed at the enormous white dome facing us. Like the goddess Poli'ahu with her cloak removed, the observatory was exposed, in full view; the metal shell was drawn back, open for the ceremony. There were several other observatories as well, staking out their piece of the sky from the mountaintop. The van came slowly to a halt and the driver instructed us, 'Step out very slowly. If you don't, you may have a nasty surprise.' I felt like leaping out, but I stepped down slowly, as if on alien soil. It was what I imagined walking in space

Volcanic Visions

to be like – surrounded by phosphorescent sky, the ether went straight to the head. High on *prana*,* I walked into the dome.

Outside, I had been stunned by the pristine atmosphere and hadn't noticed the chill. Inside, however, the first thing I was aware of was the cold. The frigid air, contained, with no brilliant sunlight to dissipate the frost, sucked up my bodily warmth; my teeth began to chatter. Amid the crowd of heavily clad people, hugging themselves to regain the heat that had been siphoned off, there was a palpable air of excitement.

A project scientist demonstrated the work of the giant computer, his voice hollow under the colossal metal shell. I jotted down a few notes, but focused on observing the awesome technology. After several astronomers and government dignitaries had made speeches, cameras began flashing wildly. I blindly took pictures with my 35-mm camera. Prince Philip stood smiling on the podium while Governor Waihee's wife placed a lei around his neck. Without a word the Prince unveiled the dedication plaque of the James Clerk Maxwell Telescope and stepped back to join Lord Buxton, who was also in a thin suit mute under the icy dome, looking as if he too was bitten by the Snow Queen.

As if to dispel the freeze, the *kahuna* priest, Father La Costa, entered wearing long robes, a thick ti leaf adorning his neck. Ordained a Catholic priest as well as a *kahuna*, he was a representative of Christian and shamanic traditions. Spraying holy water from a large ti leaf he held, he blessed the new telescope.

After the dedication ceremony, which provided less drama than I had anticipated, the telescope itself was center stage. I went on a tour of the observatory and met Professor Longair, Astronomer Royal for Scotland. I asked him what he considers to be the philosophical significance of viewing the origins of the universe. With enthusiasm, he gave me his view: 'Molecular clouds are the birthplaces of stars. To understand galaxies we must understand the origins of the stars, which leads to an understanding of our own origins. Although the "Big Bang" left footprints in the millimeter

---

Prana: literally, vital air; the subtle energy that is present in the breath, in every cell in the body and in a universal or atmospheric energy.

background fifteen billion years ago, the telescope does not make maps of the whole picture directly. Only by making one map at a time can we piece them together to make the big picture.'

Soon after the interview the press began disbanding and I went outside to join my party. As I stepped out of the metal shell, I stumbled, and realized that it had been a long time since I had felt my feet.

On the drive back to Hilo I was still feeling transported, and reflected that although seeing the Prince and attending the dedication ceremony was what had drawn me to Mauna Kea, it had been a peak experience for many reasons. The rarefied atmosphere, the chemistry of the people I interacted with, the anticipation and excitement of the gathering, and the mystique of the myth of Poli'ahu, goddess of the snows and guardian of Mauna Kea, all contributed in some way to feeling altered by having been to the mountaintop.

At home that evening I noted that my ears rang loudly from the change in altitude, and I had a dream that revealed I had been affected on a subliminal, as well as conscious, level by the journey to Mauna Kea. My mouth was wide open and many bees were busily gathering nectar from the back of my throat. When the bees departed to gather nectar elsewhere, they left behind their husks, or shed skins. I spat out the husks matter-of-factly, but continued to taste the nectar dripping down my throat.

On one level the dream was straightforward, recalling the sentiment of my experience that day. I had gone to see the Prince and, in the process had enjoyed the camaraderie of the astronomers and reporters I had met. When the visitors departed, they left behind the husks, or memories, of that event. On another level, however, the dream was perhaps communicating that I had been affected by the cosmic rays that were perceptible at the 13,000-foot altitude atop Mauna Kea. The energy stimulated the production of etheric fluid from my pineal gland and was providing nourishment on an esoteric level.

The next night I had another dream with a similar metaphoric theme. Outside, children were playing on dirt mounds. Digging in the dirt, they found several skeletons. One child unearthed a skeleton that he identified as mine, and handed it to me. The body frame was all there, but the neck and cranial bones were missing. An elixir was dripping down a filmy area in the space that would correspond to a throat, which I interpreted as being my subconscious. 'I'm not a paleontologist,' I said. 'I don't dig up bones.' The dream showed me the physical frame as a staircase or vessel and conductor of etheric fluid. The mound symbolized the Earth, which like the body, is a temple or storage area for the sacred orgone energy.

I reflected on the contents of the dreams and the effect on the psyche of having journeyed to one of the highest places on Earth. The magnetic and cosmic energy radiating from that power spot stimulates an evolutionary activity within the subconscious mind, which stores information within its data bank for further use and growing awareness.

Reading through the *Hilo Tribune Herald* over the next few days, I discovered that not all the visitors to the mountain were equally transported. Prince Philip, a long-time aviator, was quoted as saying, 'I'm convinced that the only place man should be at 14,000 feet is in the pressurized cabin of an airplane.'* I wondered if anyone had suggested that he wear a heavy coat and if he had acclimated at the midpoint before ascending the mountain. Perhaps he was displeased because he had made the journey out of duty rather than in response to a mythic script.

On a vision quest the hero experiences a 'calling'. The seeker prepares for the journey and, like Moses, is called to the 'mountaintop', a sacred place in which to open consciousness beyond finite perception. In contrast to his father's rejection of the mythic journey, Prince Charles was receiving news coverage because he was spending time in Scotland tending the sheep by day and sleeping on the dirt floor in a peasant hut by night. Enduring the label 'the lone loon', this prince was seeking his own mythology, independent of the family script, long enough to hear his own heart beat, to look at the stars and to touch the Earth.

After attending the dedication ceremony on Mauna Kea, I registered for the International Geology Conference, held at the University of Hawaii, Hilo, which provided the opportunity to understand

---

Hilo Tribune Herald, April 28, 1987.

Genesis

more about the origins of the Hawaiian volcano. Most of the attention was given to Kilauea, which has been the most active and predictable volcano on our planet in modern times, providing scientists with an understanding of the forces active in the Earth's interior. Looking into the magma pool of the newest fissure, they can see reflected the alchemical workings of the universe, the microcosmic vision of genesis reflected in the caldera mirror.

One of the most fascinating lectures I attended at the conference centered around Loihi, a submarine volcanic seamount developing off the southeast coast of the Big Island. Loihi will possibly be the next island in the Hawaiian chain. Fresh pillow lava, sheet and lobate flows, *aa* lava and *pahoehoe* issue from the summit of this baby volcano situated on the hot spot from which all the islands in the chain developed.

Later, I again contemplated the similarity between the volcanic system and *kundalini*. Like volcanoes that form along the hot spots on the royal line of the Ring of Fire, the *chakras*, or energy vortices in the body, are situated along the etheric royal line of the *kundalini*. When heat runs through the *kundalini*, from its source at the base of the spine, the *chakras* open as individual volcanic vortices. As macro- and microcosmic mandalas reflecting the origins of the universe and our planet, the volcanoes are also mirrors of human potential. From the Earth's core to the mountaintop, and in the body's esoteric and exoteric structure, there is an inherent DNA code that, when pieced together, creates the big picture of the universe.

Journeying to Hawaii had brought me to Mauna Kea, a sky mandala reflecting the Earth's star origins. It had brought me to Kilauea, which, in its bubbling caldera, mirrors the eons of evolution from the time of genesis. In our evolutionary cycle, from DNA molecule to enlightened being, we are all born from the alchemist's cauldron.

7

THE MYTH

Flowers drip in a humid atmosphere
ripe birds hop among the plants
in the orgone pulsations
of the tropical bush

a woman plucks orchids for her hair
and sends one down stream
for her waiting lover

while the wind sighs
and breathes in and out
a chlorophyll dream
in the Garden of Mu.

Upon the earth, the gods ... hankering after existence in physical bodies, became incarnated on this planet, and so became the Divine Progenitors of the human race.

Tibetan Book of the Dead*

I entered the tropical rain forest on the Hamakua coast quietly, aware of the forest spirits. Guavas and bread fruit hung from the trees and lay strewn around the forest floor. Brilliant birds hopped from bush to bush and geckos slithered among the plants. I sat on a fallen tree and breathed in the pungent scent of red earth and green wetness. Listening to the sounds of a waterfall and bird calls, I watched the sky slip by in low-flying clouds, opening into azure portholes over the garden of Mu. According to legend, the islands

---

*W. Y. Evans-Wentz (ed.), London, OUP, 1960, p. 8.

The Myth

were once connected to a large land mass called Mu, which was broken up during volcanic activity. Now they remain separate paradise worlds floating in the sea.

Further up the Hamakua coast, in Honamu, I spent some time with Ananda, in his house nestled among lush forest growth. While chanting mantra together in his shrine room I thought of the story Ananda had shared with me many years ago. In the temple where we used to live, the statue of Buddha with the soulful eyes smiled at Ananda and filled him with so much compassion that he has been consumed ever since with the desire to heal others' pain and to chant the same mantra that made Lord Buddha smile.

Ananda still had one strong worldly attachment. In a room devoted to his music, the keyboard and sound system were the oldest link to his pre-monastic days. There we sang together until the sparks flew and memories became too strong. Although we had spent time together on the island, it was different being alone in his house. I said goodbye and went back to the cool breeze along the Hamakua coast.

When I arrived at a cliff overlooking the sea along Laupahoehoe, the power and beauty of the spot moved through me as something tangible. The turquoise sea crashed against the black rocks below. The sea spirits had a song that brought back awareness of the primal body, of a soul living on the razor's edge. I wanted to remain in that relationship of the primal body, the Earth and the sea. I stood there for many minutes with my hair and dress whipping around me, feeling surcharged with the elemental power. Then a stranger came up to me and said, 'Did you know this is the spot where the tsunami took the schoolhouse full of children back to the sea?' I was stunned. 'A big one hits every twenty years. We're overdue now.'

'Morbid man,' I thought, but I could not shake the image of the children swallowed by the sea. I was angry that the spirits had the power to consume the unaware. I wanted to call back the lost children, the water babies, but it had been twenty years. I stared out at the sea and watched a particularly powerful wave crash against the rocks. I suddenly had a gripping fear that I would be swallowed up. I tried to let go of this recurring, haunting feeling by observing my breath, in and out, in and out. After several conscious repetitions, the panic subsided. I settled down and watched the rhythm of the

Volcanic Visions

waves, the ebb and the flow of emptiness and form, of life and death.

A subtle change in the climate on the island heralded the arrival of spring, and with it the Little League season. The games on Hawaii had a slightly different flavor than the ones I had watched the six previous years in California. The kids' names were lyrical and it was a pleasure hearing the coaches call out, 'Hit 'em, Kalani!' 'Can do, Uta!' At the snack bar refreshments included exotic tropical fruit drinks and salty, sour and bitter savories imported from Japan, as well as the usual hot dogs, ice cream and cola.

Along with the other parents on the bleachers, I cheered and made a lot of noise, intermittently exchanging kid lore. I split my attention during the games, trying to be attentive to each play and the score of the game, and to conversations with other parents. I was also aware of the surroundings – the red earth, the warm pikake-scented air and the sinuous, swaying trees surrounding the field.

I began sitting with the same two moms, Rachel, a commercial photographer, and Ann, a full-time mom and wife of a military man stationed on Mauna Kea's flanks. At first we talked about practical things, like how to get the iron-rich, bleach-resistant dirt out of our kids' baseball uniforms. A few weeks into the season the scope of our conversations broadened and Ann talked about her explorations on the island, in which she and her three kids searched for artifacts and traces of monuments left by the Meneheunes.

According to folklore, the Meneheunes were the first people on Mu, and are sometimes referred to simply as the Mu. After the cataclysm and submergence of the great continent, the surviving Meneheunes populated the Hawaiian islands. Later, the conquering Tahitians forced the Meneheunes to build dams, bridges, and fences – one of which Ann thought she and her kids had found. At some point the Meneheunes mysteriously disappeared from the islands without a trace, although some reports indicate a few stayed behind and live hidden in the tropical forests. Remains of their monuments have been found on the island of Kauai, and it is also rumored that the bridge that spans much of the Big Island was built by them.

The Myth

Ann's idea of exploring and mine weren't quite the same. For her, exploring ancient sites and monuments was an entertaining physical activity. In my search I employed meditative attention for a kind of psychic archeology. By the time we arrived at the Meneheune fence near the Pohakuloa army base, my interest had diminished and my psychic channels were shut tight. The kids had a good time, however, scrambling over the fence and yelling at passing army trucks.

Rachel reported to us that her guru had described Mu as it was recorded in ancient Hindu texts, and confirmed the legend that the Hawaiian islands are the mountaintops of Mu, all that remains of the continent above water. He told his students that Mu's civilization flourished in a golden age in which the vibratory rate on the planet was at its apex. Although that era was long past, the islands retained a vibration cultivated when advanced mystical practices were mastered. And, according to the same teacher, although the planet is at its lowest point in the present Kali Yuga, or age of iron, we are soon to enter a 2,000-year mini golden age, during which many people will experience an enhanced compassion and spiritual mastery.

I felt viscerally, as well as intuitively, that I had found the myth I had come to the island to unravel – the buried memories of the lost continent of the Pacific.

Soon after talking to Rachel, I met someone who told me of the existence of a pyramid temple hidden in the rain forest. I immediately wondered if the temple was a monument surviving the destruction of Mu. I was not prepared to go on a major expedition just then, so I put that quest on the back burner and began my search for texts tracing the Hawaiians back to the lost continent.

*Tales of the Night Rainbow*** records an oral history of several families on Molokai who trace their lineage to the Meneheune. Pali Lee, an elder on Molokai, refers to aloe-leaf scrolls found by Herman Cortés in a small village in Mexico.† The scrolls contained charts, stories and descriptions of Mu, revealing that the inhabitants used

---

*Pali Lee and Koko Willis, *Tales of the Night Rainbow*, Honolulu, Night Rainbow Publishing Co., 1987.
†ibid., p. 108.

Volcanic Visions

mental powers to help with their work, and lived in a state of balance and respect for all the life forms around them. An apparent survivor from Mu also recorded in the scrolls that the continent was decimated by volcanic eruptions, earthquakes and floods.

Lee and Willis also mention an unpublished manuscript by Solomon Kaulili that refers to some of the clans of Mu retained in the oral history, including the shark, the owl, eel, pig, thunder and lightning.* I was intrigued at the mention of the shark clan, because it gave me the first clue as to the implications of a dream I had had three years before. On my return to California after my first trip to Hawaii, I dreamt that my son and I arrived on the island by small boat. We got to shore and made our way through the forest in search of the people with whom we were going to stay. All around us was a thick, misty swamp with low palms and waist-high ferns. I knew the ancients were there and felt a haunting familiarity with the landscape. A man of small stature suddenly came forward and said, 'Welcome to the shark clan.' I didn't understand why he identified us with his clan, but was glad that he recognized and welcomed us. Reading about the shark being one of the family totems on Mu, I thought the dream may have been indicating that I had a past-life affiliation with that *aumakua*.

In my search to discover more about the beginnings of Mu, I came upon a text called *The Kumulipo*, translated by Leinani Melville.† This work contains the creation chants passed down through the generations, which describe the origins of the first humans:

> The spirit of a child descended from the Holy Mother Uri.
> At that time the souls of future human beings were created by the thousands in the Spiritual Country of God.
> That child came . . . [in]
> The breath of our guardian and protector from whom the blood of mankind descended . . .

---

*ibid., p. 107.
†Leinani Melville, *Children of the Rainbow*, Wheaton, Ill., Theosophical Publishing House, 1969.

The Myth

> To be born from their mother who was to give them birth on earth.
>
> Rai Rai, the royal lady from Po, who came here from her distant homeland in space . . .
>
> She was sent to deliver unto being upon this earth the human beings who were soon to blossom as branches of the Tree of Life in Po.*

According to the chants the Meneheunes knew their motherland by several names, including Ta Rua, Tahiti, Mu, Havaii and Havaiiki. 'Ha' refers to the breath, 'Vai' indicates water, and Havaii therefore describes the moisture that cooled the steamy terrain of Mu after the creation of our planet.†

In the Hawaiian cosmology‡ Io is the one god without beginning or end. Io's first progeny included Kane, the god of light, the most important of the deities, who was considered the originator and god of culture. Second was Ku, the god of stability, the architect in the work of creation. Third was Lono, the god of sound, the builder, the deity who ruled the storms and cloud signs. Then there was Kanaloa, the god of the sea, considered by some mythologists to have been a satan, who ruled a corrupt humankind after the spiritual 'fall' in the first civilization on Mu.

Kane married the goddess Uri, who gave birth to Rai Rai, a goddess and the first woman on Earth, who, in turn, gave birth to humans. Her descendants populated Mu, the first land to cool after creation. Ku married Haumea the goddess of Earth and fire, who gave birth to many children, including Pele. All of Haumea's children are *aumakuas* – ancestral spirits and the heads of spirit families, who can be petitioned as protectors by humans who are members of their respective clans – and are referred to interchangeably as deities and spirits.

---

*ibid., pp. 78–9, 84.
†ibid., p. 8.
‡Johannes E. Anderson, *Myths and Legends of the Polynesians*, Tokyo, Charles E. Tuttle Co., 1969, p. 394.

Volcanic Visions

In Pele's immediate family, her sister Hi'iaka, the spirit of the dance, is her favorite. Then there is Laka, the goddess of fertility, who in one of her aspects is a peaceful spirit and also an embodiment of dance. In another, she becomes Kapo, a goddess of sorcery and sexual power who can shapeshift into any desired form. Her sister Namakaokahai is the goddess of the sea and Pele's rival. Pele has one mortal sister, Ka'ohelo, who was transformed into a 'ohelo shrub when she died. She grows along the volcano's flanks and flowers into little red berries, which are sacred to Pele.

Pele's five brothers represent the spirit of thunder, the spirit of explosion, the rain of fire, and the fire spears – the projectiles breaking through fissures during volcanic eruptions. Her favorite, Kamohoali'i, at times takes on the form of a man and, at others, becomes the king of sharks, a powerful ally for Hawaiian families in his totem.

In the myths about the guardians of the heavenly worlds, some, 'who flew through the firmament in pearly shells or sailboats fashioned from billowy clouds',* were assigned to attend to the spiritual development of Earth's children:

> Forty souls of young gods were breathed into being as the stars were born, and they were to become the planetary lords of the stars, after which they were named ... They were assigned to earth as instructors, to teach Kane's children his sacred commandments. It was their duty to point the way to the illumined spiral staircase ... Once their missions were accomplished on earth ... their souls flew away to the stars whose names they bore.†

The reference to the 'pearly shells' made me think that, perhaps, it is not coincidental that flying saucers have frequently been sighted hovering within clouds, appearing as if fashioned from the clouds themselves, while the reference to the illumined spiral staircase was

---
*Melville, op. cit., p. 47.
†ibid.

The Myth

to me reminiscent of the dream I had had in which elixir dripped down into my skeletal 'staircase', which houses the spiral movement of the *Kundalini*.

In the oral history collected by Martha Beckwith, anthropologist Mary Kuwena Pukui said:

> They say that in ancient times the gods came to Hawaii from overseas with their families and followers, and peopled the group. Up to that time, only spirits dwelt here. For a long time they lived with their people as visible, personal gods, but when they became disgusted with their evil ways they left them, and went elsewhere. But they left a promise that someday they would return in diminutive size and speaking strange tongues so that the people would not recognize them.*

The reference to diminutive gods who would return to the planet reminded me of 'contact' stories in which people have reported seeing and interacting with aliens of small stature, about three feet high, according to some sources.

The Hawaiian myths tell that the heavenly worlds cultivated by the gods and humans on Mu survived for many millennia, but eventually the evil thoughts and actions of humans resulted in an unleashing of destructive forces in the environment, bringing the corrupted civilization to an end.

An apocalyptic verse in *The Kumulipo* states.

> Man has become evil . . .
> Born was evil . . .
> Born were noises bursting in the air, explosions from volcanoes that blew the earth to pieces.
> Ta Rua [Mu] disintegrated and sank lower and lower into the eddying sea while the four winds howled . . .
> The dashing water caused great sorrow, grieving, wailing, and lamenting in the eradication of mankind.†

---

*Martha W. Beckwith, *Hawaiian Mythology*, Honolulu, University of Hawaii Press, 1970, p. 85.
†Melville, *op. cit.*, p. 102.

Volcanic Visions

Even with haunting fears of being scorched by the fiery blasts of a volcano or being devoured by the sea, I was drawn like a magnet to a phantom memory in the Pacific. I was remembering, perhaps, a lifetime in which I left my motherland behind or went on down to a seething, sinking world. Called back through dreams and by volcanic fascination through the years, I returned to the mountain tops, the last vestiges of Mu, to remember a sacred world shared by the gods. I came back to Havaiiki, a reflection of Po, floating in the sea.

8

THE SCRIPT

Goddess

hear me   her own inspiration
as I stretch   on the limbs
and dangle   my head
in the cool   green leaves
and splash   my colors
for the sun
I was born
in Eden

Looking over my dream journal, I found an entry describing a woman who was writing a book about a tree that gives birth to luminous silver eggs. When fully developed, the eggs are caught up like spores and dispersed by the wind to places all around the world. Where the seed takes hold, trees grow and give birth to more 'moon' eggs.

I interpreted my dream as being a reflection of the book I came to the island to write. However, the potency of the dream lingered long after I had interpreted it, which made me think that there were other dimensions to the dream to explore. Jung said that when we are in the presence of an archetype of transformation, there are multiple levels of meaning that seem almost inexhaustible, and we uncover one level only to find another.* This was so with the symbolism of the moon-egg dream.

---

*C. G. Jung, *Collected Works*, Vol. 9, Pt 1, *Archetypes and the Collective Unconscious*, 2nd edn., Princeton, NJ, Princeton University Press, 1969.

Volcanic Visions

The moon tree indicates female generative energy, a motif of the Mother Goddess, who gives birth in a cosmic egg. According to anthropologist Monica Sjoo, soma, the mind-expanding potion, was the fruit of the moon tree.* (Eastern traditions maintain that soma, or nectar, is released from the pituitary gland in one who becomes enlightened, attaining the 'full moon' of consciousness.) The moon eggs symbolize the fecundity and 'metamorphosis, wonder-working and medicinal healing' of the Mother Goddess.†

Sjoo refers to the goddess of the underworld as the goddess of the dark side of the moon, symbolizing divination, illumination and the powers of healing. Illumination, or self-realization, results from working with the powerful and disruptive psychological aspects of the unconscious, and integrating them into the personality. Whereas previously the self turned in on itself in dualistic struggles, becoming depleted and unable to harness energy, the self integrated with the dark side has the energy and tremendous power needed to achieve illumination.

On the terrain of Pele, the Hawaiian goddess of the underworld, it is in keeping to dream of a moon tree belonging to the goddess of the dark side of the moon. Pele produces visions such as a space ship glowing like a volcanic temple, and moon eggs, lovely receptacles of nectar from the divine, disseminated around the world as agents of metamorphosis and healing.

The dream also reflects a cross-cultural origins myth in which the universe is conceived by the mother–father god and born from a cosmic egg.‡ The newborn universe eventually reaches maturation and, in a 'Big Bang', sends its spores throughout space in a continuum of evolution, in which life forms evolve in a spiral of self-awareness. The dream illustrates the rebirth of the feminine principle on our planet as the alchemical element needed for illumination and transformation.

---

*Monica Sjoo, *The Ancient Religion of the Greatest Cosmic Mother of All*, Trondheim, Norway, Rainbow Press, 1981, p. 40.
†ibid.
‡Erich Neumann, *The Great Mother*, Princeton, NJ, Princeton University Press, 1974, p. 328.

The Script

The tree is also a metaphor for the *kundalini*, which has both female and male properties within it. Specialized mystical practices unite the female and male channels of the *kundalini*, which, in its single form, becomes a golden flower, a fountain of light.* In this transmutation process cosmic consciousness and the perception of life as a whole is realized. The flowering brings a luminosity to perception. The enlightened spontaneously releases spores of spiritual essence into the atmosphere. Those who are receptive are infused with the energy and often become motivated to actively pursue a path of transformation.

According to Buddhist scripture, a Tibetan yogi named Padmasambhava demonstrated a spiritual and physical parthenogenesis when he selected the process of his own birth and emerged self-born, from a flower. When asked who his parents were, the child answered, 'My father is wisdom, and my mother is voidness ... I am here to destroy lust, anger, and sloth.'† Padmasambhava's emergence from a flower demonstrates to us metaphorically that we, too, can attain a spiritual parthenogenesis by embarking on a path of transformation, destroying within ourselves lust, anger, and ignorance. As the spiritual element develops, the practitioner experiences a flowering of the thousand-petaled lotus on the crown of the head, from which an enlightened being emerges, self-born.

One day I received an announcement in the mail about the Harmonic Convergence forecast for August 16/17, 1987. The literature explained that Mercury, Venus, Mars and Regulus would be in conjunction on this date (astronomers said it would be a week later), and this augured the beginning of a global shift into a new planetary cycle, referred to as the 'fifth world' in Hopi and Zapotec prophecies. The *Book of the Hopi* states: 'The emergence to the future fifth world has begun. You can read this in the earth itself. Plant forms from previous worlds are beginning

---

*Richard Wilhelm and C. G. Jung, *Secret of the Golden Flower: A Chinese Book of Life*, New York, Harcourt Brace Jovanovich Inc., 1962, p. 38.
†W. Y. Evans-Wentz, *Tibetan Book of the Great Liberation*, London, OUP, 1968, p. 106.

Volcanic Visions

to spring up as seeds. Seeds are being planted in the sky as stars. The same kind of seeds are being planted in our hearts.'*

A Zapotec prophecy says:

> One of the incarnations of Quetzalcoatl is buried beneath the roots of the tree [the El Tule tree in southern Mexico], and as the first rays of the dawning sun of the new heaven cycle sink into the depths of the Earth, billions of tiny spirits will burst from the heart of Quetzalcoatl. They will slowly rise through the trunk, through the limbs and branches, appearing as sparkles of light, finally erupting from every leaf and seedling, to circle the globe, each spirit to implant itself within the heart of a human being, and plant a crystal of peace and love. . . .†

In his notes for the International Sacred Sites Festival Jim Berenholtz wrote:

> The ancient prophecies of Mesoamerica pinpoint the return of Quetzalcoatl, Lord of the Dawn, to the time that correlates with August 16/17, 1987 in the Gregorian calendar . . . Quetzalcoatl lives, as potentially, a seed within each one of us. 144,000 human beings will emerge to be the sprouting of that seed on the day of Harmonic Convergence, and will grow to flower and seed again towards the awakening of all humanity in the years that follow.‡

The prophecies indicate a collective and individual myth in which we are evolving into a fifth world, where spiritual evolution and enlightenment will be the goal of our culture. In our present phase old, destructive forms of civilization are rising up before the fall, and the planet is undergoing the much-talked-about cleansing, which will eventually bring about a regenerated world, with a

---

*Frank Waters, *Book of the Hopi*, New York, Ballantine Books, 1963, p. 408.
†Jim Berenholtz, *International Sacred Sites Festival Notes*, Maui, Hawaii, 1987.
‡ibid.

The Script

higher vibratory frequency. Pioneers are finding the means for planetary and cellular regeneration in a diseased world. The late Wilhelm Reich, for example, discovered that the orgone (known to the Hindus as *prana*), the etheric life force inherent in all living things, can be harnessed to positively affect cellular and psychic transformation in the individual and, potentially, in the collective environment.

I noticed strong parallels between the metaphors in the moon-egg dream, the Native American prophecies and the Hawaiian creation myth in which 'the human beings ... were soon to blossom as branches of the Tree of Life in Po.'*

From another perspective, the moon eggs, like the seeds from the Tule tree, indicate that many of us are being seeded with an ultraterrestrial† consciousness so that we might awaken to our origins as blossoms on the tree of life from Po to come to fruition as fully enlightened beings. As individuals are infused with higher octaves of sensibility, the fourth-dimensional awareness becomes absorbed and diffused into the larger group, a movement from the personal to the collective.

The ancient prophecies, dreams, visions and myths were formulating a pattern like the multifacets of a mosaic design. I wanted to know what my archetypal role was in this collage. I wanted to know my part in the collective mythology. I searched my dreams and subconscious for answers, and looked for clues in everyday interactions and activities. I received more symbols, metaphors and hunches, but did not yet get an aerial view of the larger picture.

At the metaphysical bookstore in Kona I hoped to find some material that would speak to me, putting all the patterns and shapes into an articulate cohesive form. Flyers were posted for a medium

---

*Leinani Melville, *Children of the Rainbow*, Wheaton, Ill., Theosophical Publishing House, 1969, p. 84.

†The dictionary defines 'ultra' as 'beyond the limits of; transcending what is ordinary; on the other side of'. I define 'ultraterrestrial' as pertaining to sentient beings and a state of consciousness that is beyond the limits of three-dimensional awareness and activities, usually referring to beings who are 'on the other side' of our planet – extraterrestrial beings in some cases, ascended masters in others.

Volcanic Visions

who specialized in working with people who had had extraterrestrial experiences. Michael and Aurora El Legion, both psychics, were visiting from their Extraterrestrial Communications Center in Arizona.* Although I didn't know if dreams and feelings of transmission fit into a 'communications' category, and was skeptical that channeling could shed light on my inner mythology, I decided to indulge my fancy by finding out.

Michael and I met at a hotel in Hilo. He was probably in his mid-thirties, ordinary in appearance and manner. I noted only a large crystal around his neck. Facing each other in straight-backed chairs, we had a brief exchange. I didn't tell him much about why I was there, but primed myself to be receptive during the reading, reserving judgement until later. He informed me that he channels intergalactic beings, whose appearance resembles the human form, and that one or more of them might choose to come through him during the course of the reading. Then, as we got comfortable in our chairs, he turned on the tape recorder, using the tape I brought for the session and later transcribed.

When we were ready to begin, he shut his eyes and began an elaborate invocation of protection, calling first on the Ascended Master, Christ Jesus. My attention on Michael almost entirely disappeared as I felt a powerful force field manifest in the room. I sat forward to understand everything being said, but found a few minutes into the reading that I was sitting flush against my chair. There was a perceptible pulsation of light in the area around us as my breathing became rhythmical and deep. Waves of energy entered the room and with each breath I went into a deeper trance.

The medium's voice went through a transition and another voice identified himself as Ashtar. He told me this area (Hawaii) is where I had spent considerable time as a priestess on Mu 12,000 years ago, and had returned to restore my memory of the mysteries I practised at that time. He provided a genealogical account of my past lives. Within two hours he offered answers to my questions concerning

---

*Although the El Legions were residents of Arizona at that time, they now conduct the ET Communications Network in Malibu, California.

The Script

the incomprehensible feelings that were arising in dreams and visions. Whether fantasy or part of a transpersonal reality, he identified my part in the collective mythology.

In an ordinary state of consciousness I might have thought his words and message fantastic and even ludicrous. In the altered state brought about by the surcharged field, however, I allowed myself to respond inwardly to the things said and felt that some of them corresponded with a higher truth.

Greetings, Father–Mother God that I Am, I Am Ashtar of the Ashtar Command. I come in at this time, sister of light, to bring clarity and understanding to that of your mission. You are termed an Eagle Commanderess, which in the cosmic spheres is a title that refers to the consciousness level you brought with you in this present human embodiment.

We of the Universal Federation, the universal Christ force, are endeavoring to link the star people, the volunteers in human embodiment, together at this time. We are helping them to allow greater power on the conscious level. This is a spiritual power that was used during the priesthood in the past. For those who are of the feminine polarity, as it was in the akashic and galactic records, have been as high priestesses, and the men have been the high priest scientists. There was a certain path that they followed, though their missions and their personalities were unique, each in their own way.

This area you have come back to is what is left of Lemuria; the rest went down 12,000 years ago. This was an area where you spent considerable time in the temple as priestess.

There are many collective things that help to connect you to others who are of a similar vibration, and that is what we describe as those who speak the language of the spirit; there is a rapport and affinity between them. It's a time of reunion when the Eagles gather on the Earth level. There is great potential at this time to tap in, and to receive information in a much more direct sense from us. When we link to that brother or sister, it is for the purpose of helping you fulfill your mission, in the aspect of getting information out to others,

Volcanic Visions

because you will find the need to share with other brothers and sisters of light that you come into contact with.

As part of your heritage that you have brought with you, who you are is identified by the energy that you give off, this light, this individuality of the Divine Presence within you of the I AM THAT I AM as manifested individually through you. This energy itself is an identification like radar.

You need to bring in the more assertive aspects of yourself, allowing that creative part to express itself and bring information through. That will be of service to others who you meet along the path of life. You are being drawn forward to remember again, as it was in the council. Even though one follows many human lives, you are still technically a member of our council.

We come in over the planet observing the light that emanates from each person, and how one can increase that light and amplify it by wearing crystals, and by doing color meditation and light decrees, by watching what you are putting into your physical bodies, as well as mental and psychological attitudes. All of these things are very important, affecting one's state of being and condition upon the planet. It's all part of the awakening process and the ability to ground that light. That is why you are in the human embodiment, to be a grounder of light.

In relation to the rainbow family, the word rainbow is literally true, because, though the vast majority of us from other worlds are human appearing, as you were before taking human embodiment, there are also many blue, green and purple forms. What is important is the energy of consciousness, not the rainbow hue.

Some would describe us as etheric but that is not the proper description. I am etheric but I am also physical in the fourth and higher dimensional spheres. It is in the sixth through the twelfth dimensions that I normally spend my time. All the commanders and commanderesses are versatile. They are capable of traveling to the thirty-three dimensional spheres that we share with other planetary cultures.

Understand that when we refer to our ships, we are not

The Script

dependent upon using our ships to travel, because we can travel wherever we want in our immortal light bodies. But when groups of us travel, as you have traveled back and forth to the Pleiades, Clarion, Orion and Sirius, where you've had many incarnations, many existences, we have used our ships. You have had lifetimes of existences in which you have experienced other worlds as a member of the Federation, representing many cultures in the sense of learning and teaching. Much of that you will work to fulfill in this lifetime.

You had to learn to survive and live to the best of your ability in a three-dimensional environment. You have allergies, which for you are a symptom of being allergic to this planet. But you've been here many times on different missions. Because this is the end of a great cycle, it is much more significant how one has passed the test and has gone through the initiations – the trials and tribulations that one experiences. At times one can call it spiritual boot camp or a sense of purging by fire.

There were lifetimes when the negative forces attempted to intimidate you. It is often said that how much light one brings affects how much interference you must encounter when stirring up things in an attempt to transmute. The opposition often comes up when using all the ways and means that one has to eliminate the negativity and darkness, ignorance, tragedy and suffering.

There have been times, too, when the desire to return to us, to get away from all this, has been very strong. There are forces that made you feel that way, made you forget your mission that you volunteered to come in to do. Your work has been to help illuminate and transmute the negative forces lovingly but with firmness. You've had to learn to try to keep your sense of humor; and are still learning to laugh at times and see that this is all very limited, a very temporary period, just a flash in time. It may seem like a long time on the three-dimensional level compared to our level, as there are not the limitations on our level that there are on Earth.

We watch over our emissaries but give them a freedom of choice and sense of privacy. There is a fine line between what we can do and what we can't. I'm merely saying that we helped you help yourself to achieve the goals that would help your brothers and sisters.

Soon you will see our Mother Ship as confirmation that we are nearby and you are going to be observing our craft quite regularly until physical contact: being taken aboard our ship. That phase of mission will come about when the time is right, when the Eagles will be gathered up and returned once again to complete their mission. This was the vow, this was the pledge that the Eagle Commanders and Commanderesses will be returned to us again.

As Ashtar came to a conclusion, another being, Cassiopeia, came through with more detailed information about my life. I sat in an altered state; my body felt solid yet etheric and filled with light.

When Michael returned from trance and opened his eyes, he began to speak in a perfunctory way. He went from the sublime to the mundane in a matter of seconds. I was unnerved by the transition. My energy system was attuned to the two presences who had been in the room, who seemed dissimilar from the man in front of me.

I looked forward to going home to process the experience, and was curious to see if I looked as different as I felt. At home I looked in the mirror and noted a turquoise glow to my skin. Two lines that run down my forehead stood out clearly, as if marked by a blue pen. I interpreted the two lines as being the channels of the *kundalini*. In the third-eye area a bright red mark stood out, surrounded by a circular indentation. My eyes looked clear, radiating a knowingness that is usually hidden by constant soul-searching. It seemed that the presence of the beings channeled and the contents of the reading had activated my *kundalini*.

I continued to think about things said in the reading and still felt in a very altered state, and I sat silently in meditation for a while. I eventually was pulled back into ordinary consciousness by the sounds of women gossiping underneath my window. I thought about my son coming home from school soon, so began the conscious shift back into parenting time, with a residual transported feeling. A few minutes after the transition, Josh burst in the door

The Script

with the announcement, 'I'm home!' followed by 'Can I have something to eat?' I gave him a hug. 'Mom, you look beautiful!' he said with a grin. The doubts about the reading and feeling foolish came later. For that hour, during talk about school over peanut butter sandwiches and iced mango juice, my analyzer was on hold.

9

STAR CENTER

After the stars fall
and the Earth shakes and screams —
After volcanoes bring a roaring halt
to a secular reality —
a glowing Goddess will rise in the Pacific
a familiar star reborn.

The day after the channeled reading with 'Ashtar' and 'Cassiopeia' I thought about my impressions during the experience. What intrigued me the most was feeling an actual presence entering the room, changing the vibration around Michael and me. I was emotionally moved by the extraordinary energy field and felt a kind of recognition, or recall, of that force field.

The idea that I had previously been incarnated as a priestess on Mu was an appealing thought, and provided an explanation for why I had such a strong mystical attraction to the Big Island and excitement reading descriptions of the lost continent derived from Hawaiian oral histories and mythology. Being mediumistic could be a carry-over from a life in which channeling was part of my work. From my first trip on the Big Island I spontaneously opened the crown of my head to receive energies that I later came to intuitively identify as emanating from the celestial guardians and terrestrial volcanic deities.

It was interesting that Ashtar made reference to my having allergies and attributed them to 'being allergic to this planet'. Many people, however, are having allergic reactions to the contaminants in our food and in the environment, and most of us would prefer a world where there is a more loving planetary kinship system.

Considering Ashtar's prediction that I soon would be seeing their Mother ship and observing their craft regularly I knew that if I did have a significant sighting soon, I would be inclined to give more credence to the reading and to the possibility that intergalactic beings were present in my world. For the moment I thought that Michael was psychic enough to pick up on some of my own thought patterns, including those about being from another time and place. What I had no logical explanation for, however, was the perception of a powerful energy field surrounding us after the reading began and my feeling of affinity with it.

The information I received in the reading stimulated my imagination and what psychic propensities I may have. For the next few days I was absorbed in writing what I perceived to be channeled information. When I was receiving psychic input, I experienced a dimension of reality that I felt had always been with me. However, out of trance I fluctuated between validating my psychic process and the content of the channelings, and rejecting my thoughts and feelings as fantasy. I noticed that validating the experience, I felt empowered and full of energy. Conversely, when I denied its validity, I became 'beached'. Ignoring my own radar, or inner guidance system, I was floundering, lethargic and powerless. The push–pull between giving myself permission to record the channelings and damming the flow resulted in more uncomfortable repercussions: I began having blinding headaches and intense pressure in my third eye.

While I was going through this process Ananda asked me if he could connect me to a friend of his who was a scientist and philosophically oriented. He told me his friend was single, and he thought we might have some interests in common. I was preoccupied with my writing, but told him offhandedly it would be all right to give Ryan Parish my number.

The next Sunday I wrote several pages of what seemed to be transmitted material about the lost continent of Mu. According to my transcriptions, the Earth's magnetic surface is most accelerated over hot spots, where psychic events and extraterrestrial visitations are frequent and the Earth's *kundalini* is most aroused. Hot spots are the solar plexus points that maintain the necessary balance of terrestrial and cosmic energies to regenerate the Earth: without them, the planet would become demagnetized and lifeless. The civilization of Mu advanced greatly because it was situated on the royal line of

Volcanic Visions

the Ring of Fire, one of the world's key conduits of magnetic regeneration. At pivotal points of the year, when the planets and constellations were in designated alignment, the gods and goddesses met with the shaman rulers and female and male priests of Mu. I could imagine the progenitors dining, enjoying the sumptuous fruits of paradise. Lord Kane and Lady Na'Vahine, Lord Lono and Lady Rata, Lord Kanarao and Lady Hina, Lord Ku and Lady Tapo descended from the higher realms of space and toasted this tropical heaven, which they had seeded with their own progeny. I envisioned whales and dolphins sporting in the shimmering sea, free from any violation from humanity, communicating telepathically with the guardians. In the accelerated environment along the Ring of Fire, and with divine relations, the citizens of Mu flourished in a civilization created from a spiritual technology.

The temples were at the epicenter of the culture, the source of energy and power on which it depended and thrived. Inside, the female and male priests engaged in rituals prescribed by the guardians for alignment and balance within the culture and each individual. In deep trance, they opened their crown *chakras* to receive intuitive spiritual and civic guidance for the community.

The technology was based on the electromagnetic energy of the volcanoes and the stars and the temples were specially positioned to receive shafts of light aligned with the magnetic surface to facilitate a transmutation of energy in the rooms. This took place in volcanically charged transmutation chambers in which bioplasmic energy was gathered, stored and accelerated.

These chambers were used for several purposes. Adepts who were physically, emotionally and psychically prepared to undergo transmutation entered them for initiation rites. They experienced a subtler perception of reality as their cellular structure underwent a change and they obtained a light body that enabled them to travel to different dimensions and interplanetary destinations. The chambers were also used to increase the potency and efficacy of medicines, elixirs, gems and crystals.

When an untimely death interrupted a spiritual adept's transmutation process, spiritual instruction took place in a cryonic suspension chamber. While the person was suspended between lifetimes, priests worked with him or her on the etheric plane to complete initiation, thus bypassing the need to reincarnate into a new human form and begin instruction anew.

From the window of my imagination, via transmission or from past-life memory, I saw womb chambers in the temple, with doors leading to and from other worlds. The chambers were used for different rites of passage, including ritual love-making in which the woman and man used visualization to bring an evolved being into the woman's womb. Specialized mantras and visioning techniques were used to attract a baby being who was destined to work for the spiritual development of the culture.

The *aumakua* practice was another way in which divine beings incarnated in human form. A woman was courted in her dreams by a god, who eventually inseminated her. The child born from the union inherited some of the traits of its divine progenitor. (After receiving the channeled information, I later read that 'Women were supposed to be visited in a dream by *aumakua* spirits who wished to have a child by them. The dream would continue until the birth of the first child, and to this child the father would give a name.'*)

According to the transmission I was receiving, the cosmic-terrestrial religion of Mu, the balance between the lightning and serpent powers, and the heavenly and terrestrial energies of body, Earth and cosmos were worked with and utilized for consciousness expansion and for balance between living organisms. The progenitors revealed to their descendants knowledge about the body as a receptacle for the cosmos. They disseminated information on how to receive cosmic intelligence and guidance through the porthole in the crown of the head, and how to communicate with the solar system in the body that is set in motion through etheric winds, or *prana*.

It came to me that these were teachings as they were on Mu, and as they continue to be wherever there is a conscious universe. However, on Mu, as later on Atlantis, destructive priests seized the ancient science of life and twisted it into a murderous force to

---

*Martha W. Beckwith, *Hawaiian Mythology*, Honolulu, University of Hawaii Press, 1970, p. 135.

Volcanic Visions

enhance their own energy. The priests sacrificed living beings to eke out their life force, and siphoned off the orgone essence of the planet to become all-powerful. On Mu and Atlantis the Earth vomited up these ignorant ones, and then convulsed and seethed in the most violent eruptions ever known to humankind. Mu sank into the Pacific; Atlantis sank below millions of tons of volcanic ash. Those who did not learn their lessons during the last cataclysms are incarnate in the twentieth century, retaining a cannibalistic world view, systematically extracting the life energy from vulnerable peoples, from the animals, the seas, the earth, the sky. They take all and leave refuse in return.

The Hawaiian islands are, perhaps, among the last vestiges of Mu, holding wisdom secrets from the first civilization of humankind. It is of great importance that Hawaii attains a sanctuary status, exempt from exploitive activities that would release pollutants into the air, earth and water, and that we maintain its sanctity by allowing only those works and activities that are in alignment with the spiritual forces present there. The goddess Pele and the denizens of Po are the inherent rulers and guardians of the land. People with a spiritual view of the Big Island have taken political action against environmentally hazardous projects in concern for the possible desecration of Pele's home. Some fear that if her sanctuary is disturbed and defiled, there will again be volcanic activity of cataclysmic proportions. Over the last several millennia the keepers of the island have preserved the balance between themselves and Pele by maintaining respect for the environment and by giving attention due the goddess in ritual offering.

This glimpse into Mu through my channeled writings, coupled with legend, inspired thoughts of a new world based on sacred principles, as in the beginning of civilization when humanity burned with a spiritual fire and lived close to the progenitors in interdimensional time. Contemplating the material on ancient Mu, I thought about the predictions for its resurrection at the cusp of the twenty-first century. Edgar Cayce predicted a pole shift and lands appearing in the Pacific, while the Lemurian Fellowship has indicated that spiritual communities are to be built around the world, and a light center on a Pacific island will be 'the first city of the new

Star Center

Golden Age'.[*] The phoenix continent and new community will announce the end of the fourth world and Piscean Age, and greet the arrival of the fifth world and Aquarian Age. Whether or not the prophecies come true, Mu is a light center that was, that exists in remnants today and will possibly be born again, shaped according to our visions.

We each have our part in the creation of civilization and a vision to bring to pass. I had sight of mine in 1984, in a dream, soon after I first visited the Big Island. I stood on a cliff on the Hamakua coast overlooking the sea and without forethought, leapt off the cliff, my arms extended as I swooped over the Pacific islands. Exhilarated at the expanse of sky and sea, I soared over the aquamarine water and sighted a golden temple with a spire jutting into the sky from a volcanic island below. I recognized the temple and knew it to be a creation of extraterrestrials. Now, three years later, I had learned about the guardians of Mu, and the dream conjured up ideas for the creation of a temple of light powered by a spiritual technology, as it was on Mu.

In the Aquarian Age there will be the widespread use of magnetism and bioplasm. Cellular and psychic transformation, fourth-dimensional awareness, inner and outer space travel, as well as extraterrestrial and interdimensional communications, will preoccupy scientists and mystics alike. A Star Center for Extraterrestrial Studies and Interdimensional Flight might find a natural home in the volcanic terrain of the Big Island, where the electromagnetic energies of Earth and sky are accelerated. It could be created to reflect the spiritual technology of the temples of Mu, and become a light beacon in the fifth world.

Ideally, the Star Center will be housed on a spot selected by geomancers, where the solar and terrestrial forces are in correct alignment for the spiritually based technology. The building design might be likened to a circular UFO, with a crystal dome overhead. Within the solar-heated center, I imagine simple esthetic instruction rooms, with furniture made of natural products.

---

[*] David Hatcher Childress, *Lost Cities of Ancient Lemuria and the Pacific*, Stelle, Ill., Adventures Unlimited Press, 1987, p. 352.

Volcanic Visions

Courses at the Star Center will include exobiology, astrophysics and astronomy, examining non-linear world views and paradigms that might be encountered in meetings with extraterrestrials. Studies of symbolic anthropology assist in understanding possible similarities and dissimilarities in symbolic abstractions and meanings in terrestrial and extraterrestrial societies. Considering cross-cultural perspectives of extraordinary realities open the space researcher to concepts that might be outside his or her regular framework and field of perception. In-depth psychic and healing classes help the researcher to develop empathic and altered perceptual fields of awareness, which will be needed when 'making contact'. Remote viewing, a technique developed at the Stanford Research Institute, assists in expanding the researcher's long-distance clairvoyance.* Training in extraterrestrial anthropology and archeology prepares archeologists for excavations on other planets as well as for expeditions on the Pacific islands to search for surviving monuments and artifacts of Mu.

A crystal pyramid chamber will be designed as an inner-space environment to collect and heighten the psychic and physical energies of astral and interdimensional voyagers. Here multisensory modalities augment structural changes in consciousness. Selected colors, sounds, scents, massage and hypnosis deepen receptivity to innerspace communication and further astral projection. Small kivas, mounds and womb chambers provide entry stations to the subtler dimensions as, in the tradition of shamanic initiation through the millennia, the darkness of the Earth's womb has facilitated interdimensional flight. In the amniotic darkness of flotation pools filled with lotus flowers the mystic dreamer slips away. As I wrote one day after swimming in the Wailuku River: My body is an organic spaceship providing a protective skin adapted to this atmosphere. By day I move through time in an upright position, making adjustments to match the vibratory rate of those around me. But in the darkness I slip out to other dimensions in time.

---

*Russell Targ and Keith Harary, *The Mind Race: Understanding and Using Psychic Abilities*, New York, Villard Books, 1984.

10

ACCELERATION

With my love I want to consume
the earth and sky
in an explosion
of rocks and fire

. . . as it is . . . my passion is flowing
down in continuous streams
from the magma pool that is building up
inside of me

After writing for several hours, I sat back in the chair to stretch. The phone rang. The loud, insistent ring indicated a strong, masculine energy behind the call. It was Ananda's friend, Ryan Parish. He told me a little bit about the scientific research he was engaged in, and was interested in hearing about my writing. I told him about my first book, in which I interviewed shaman women, but told him nothing about my book-in-progress, as I assumed he would think it too offbeat. However, just a few minutes into the conversation Ryan asked me something that surprised me so much I almost dropped the phone: 'Are you having extraterrestrial experiences?' There were no preliminaries, no lead-ins to the question. It occurred to me that perhaps he was psychic and had picked up on the energy I was channeling when he called.

Although I had never discussed this facet of myself with Ananda, I told Ryan that I had an interest in extraterrestrial communication and was receiving inspiration in my writing that seemed to be coming from an outside source or from a past-life memory, if he believed in that kind of thing. The timing of his question unnerved me, but triggered enthusiasm. 'I was just writing about the function of an acceleration chamber as it was used in the temples of Mu,' I told him.

'That is *very* interesting,' he said. 'I have an acceleration chamber in my home.'

My first thought was that he made up his response on the spot, but I realized he was too sophisticated for a charade. I was intrigued and wanted to know more about Ryan Parish. He told me he wanted to explore our connection in person, so we made a date to meet.

The next Friday evening, in a quiet Japanese restaurant near the bay, I had little interest in my tempura. Ryan was focusing all his attention on me and his eyes seemed to be boring holes into my head. I tried to assess him in a less obtrusive way. He was tall, tan, with light-brown hair, keenly intelligent dark eyes, and an authoritative, cold, steely air. I didn't talk about my transmission process nor the extraterrestrial connection. Over several small cups of sake and maneuvering chopsticks, dipping batter-fried shrimp into horse-radish and soy sauce, we studied each other without talking much. While we were finishing a last cup of rice wine a colleague of Ryan's came in and they had a quick exchange about a recent research project.

As we were getting up Ryan drew closer to me across the table to tell me how he was looking forward to my seeing his acceleration chamber. We drove first to his office, where he wanted to pick up something. The research facility was clinical and sterile, but on the walls of Ryan's office hung Balinese shadow puppets of characters from the *Ramayana* as well as Indonesian masks of deities and demons created for ritual trance dances. I appreciated his cultural and artistic sensibilities and only wished I could fathom what was so very mysterious about him.

During the drive to his house I felt somewhat apprehensive, uncomfortable about the unknown source of his intensity and some of the cryptic things he had said at dinner. When he reached his home, I felt I had already surrendered my fate by going with him and tried to put aside my uncertainty. He wanted to sit in the kitchen, sharing incidental things, as if he were stalling for something. Even at this point neither of us approached the subjects that had brought about our meeting. On my part it was because I was overwhelmed by his presence, which seemed bigger than life and was in my psychic space. Then, as if it were all according to plan,

Acceleration

Ryan suddenly reached for my hand, saying, 'It's time.' He led me out of the house, past the deck and hot tub to the garage. For a moment as he turned the doorknob I panicked: I was on the alert for anything.

I stumbled over an unseen step into the room and looked around, goose bumps on my arms. The room was bathed in violet and magenta light and etheric space music seemed to filter through every wall, adding to the eerie beauty. On the floor was a transparent globe with violet and magenta lightwaves pulsating in time to the music. But what I saw in the middle of the room almost made me drop my socks: I was staring at a large, circular UFO-shaped structure approximately three and half feet tall, with smooth sloping sides and a silvery matt finish. Levers protruded from the interior on the sloping surface. I went over and read the names inscribed over the levers, including: Pleiades, Andromeda and Orion. It was what I imagined a UFO control panel would look like, based on a dim recollection of sci-fi movies from my childhood, in which they showed the control area of a space ship.

On a couch beneath a beautiful tapestry, facing the space panel, I then joined Ryan, feeling the transportive effect of the music and lights. There were many questions, but I put them aside, allowing the mood to lull me. At one point we both turned and stared into each other's eyes, both sending and receiving transmitted thoughts. I wasn't certain why we were engaging in this ritual together, but there seemed to be some reason for our meeting and the way we communicated.

Then Ryan asked me to join him for a dip in the hot tub and we went out again into the night where he immediately took off his clothes and immersed himself in the whirling pool. I looked down at the bubbling water. Not knowing whether he would expect me to be intimate, I told him I had to wear 'something'. Ryan got out of the tub and came back with a long t-shirt. In the water it floated around my neck to which Ryan responded by reaching out, pulling me towards him, running his body over mine. I pushed away, but he took my hands and held on to them as I lay suspended on the water.

I was aroused by the night and the bubbling warm water, and my mind turned to the man 'on the other side of the world'. Looking up at the black sky and bright stars, I felt as if I were traveling

Volcanic Visions

through space, the sensation augmented by the bubbling of the water beneath me.

Still holding my hands, Ryan whispered, 'What do you see, Michele? – Tell me.'

He wanted me to be an oracle, but I was silent, not wanting to reveal more until I knew the man who invited me there. After we dressed, I asked him questions for the first time.

Sitting on the couch, Ryan fingered a chess piece on the coffee table. 'Michele, I don't do things in a logical way any more, outside of my work, which demands so much. I'm involved with intensive research, often long after regular hours. So when I come home and relax, spending time with friends, I let things evolve, without a pre-set program. I've had a lot of surprises that way. As in our first conversation on the phone: I knew there was something interesting going on with you. I didn't question my intuition, but followed it. I didn't invite you here to hustle you. I just wanted to get to know who you are without probing you with a lot of questions.'

'You probed me psychically.'

'That wasn't intentional. I guess when I go about a thing I'm very intense. I just wanted to get in there. Get to know who you are.'

'Hmmm. And why did you ask me on the phone if I had extraterrestrial experiences?'

'As I told you when we spoke on the phone, there was a quality in your voice that intrigued me. I felt you had a lot of information, and what came to mind is that the source is extraterrestrial.'

'You got that from a voice?'

'Yes,' he said. 'And what's interesting to me is that this conversation wouldn't have taken place a year ago. Before then, my focus was on my work and my social life. But then my interests outside of work went through a shift. For no known reason I became extremely interested in the metaphysical and wanted answers on all levels for the workings of the spiritual dimension. I've been doing a lot of reading in this area, as well as talking to friends who have done more exploration than I.'

'I'm still curious about why you created a control panel that looks like it belongs inside a UFO and how it functions as an acceleration chamber.'

Acceleration

'The idea of creating a sound system in a UFO-shaped panel just came to me. The room functions as an acceleration chamber, combining the sound system with a machine I'm working on that alters brain patterns. I'll show you when you feel more comfortable with me.'

I was captivated by Ryan, but I realized I had an issue of trusting a man whom I barely knew to play with my consciousness. But on some level I knew that experiences can alter our viewpoints and perceptions without our necessarily being in conscious agreement. Perhaps there was a subliminal recognition between us, as for people renewing a past-life association. According to the Ashtar reading, women descendants of the Eagle Confederation incarnated in the role of priestess, and the male descendants became priest–scientists. I wondered if Ryan was an associate from Mu. Fun thought.

The next morning, when we talked, I felt much warmer towards him, as if he were someone with whom I had survived an ordeal. I asked if my son could see the UFO sound room. Ryan set up a time for the three of us to meet.

That evening I took out my dream diary, and found an entry for one particularly interesting dream that I had had within a month of our arrival on the island. Hilo had been immersed in 'vog' that entire month, as bad as L.A. at its worst and I had been to see James West, an allergist, to treat me for a reaction to the volcanic fumes. In my dream Colleen, an artist friend, wore a silver neckpiece on which there was a dome-shaped head with large, moving eyes. In a strange way the face resembled that of Dr West. Colleen told me that it was the face of an ET and with it she could call down a 'Mother Ship'.

The neckpiece intrigued me. Josh traded something he owned for an identical piece and gave it to me as a gift. Delighted, I held the eccentric piece in my hand and focused on calling down a UFO, as Colleen had suggested. I scanned the sky, and within moments a bronze-colored disk catapulted down in my direction. 'I can't believe it! Some imagination!' I said out loud. Colleen stood next to me, watching the disk. 'How could you invalidate what's happening?' she asked.

I tried to go further, by bringing the vehicle close. As if in response to my thoughts, the disk swooped by. At close range it looked like a giant manta ray, its body supple, flexed and alive.

Volcanic Visions

I contacted a friend in California about the sighting. Elizabeth's response was that she couldn't relate to UFOs and didn't want to discuss the subject. I was disappointed, but put my mind on other things. She and I were going on a double date and were planning to meet the men at her house. In the dream her home had natural redwood floors and walls – quite different from her real home. When the two men arrived, they looked like summer, up-beat, bronzed, with natty clothes.

Supposedly a double date, we had a change of plans. Elizabeth and John took off in the car, while Gabriel and I went for a walk down a hill, almost gliding over soft grass and leaves. There was such high color and a healthful glow to his cheeks. The light from the sun was delicate and warm, softly illuminating the landscape. When I glanced at him a while later, the peach color had faded from his cheeks, replaced by a strange sheen. He was not as he appeared, I thought, but an extraterrestrial. For some inexplicable reason I stumbled forward into Gabriel's arms, and rolled with him down the hill. I was exhilarated and he also seemed to delight in the experience, as if everything was going according to plan. Later, however, when I went home, I felt dizzy and disoriented, probably from spinning down the hill.

In the next sequence of the dream I went with my son to a school open house where the kids were putting on a performance. I tried giving the show my full attention, but was so uncomfortable from the dizziness, I had trouble sitting up. Instead of dissipating, the vertigo seemed to be intensifying. By the time it was my son's turn to perform, I was completely preoccupied with the discomfort and had difficulty focusing my full attention on him.

After the show, I thought about contacting Elizabeth again. Because we shared many paranormal incidents on our spiritual paths in the past, I thought she would understand. Even though she had already told me she couldn't relate to UFOs I felt that she would be able to see the correlation of the 'others' to the spiritual teachers and higher planes. When I got to her house, I was appalled because she was abrupt, so unlike her usual demeanor. She said she was on her way out and couldn't talk. I stumbled out the door like someone drunk, and returned home feeling dizzy, alienated and frightened.

When I wakened, at first I was relieved to surface from the

dream. Then I was conscious of still being very dizzy. I checked in with myself to see if I was ill. There was no fever, no aches, no pains, no earaches or stuffy sinuses. I was dismayed, however, that I could barely lift my head off the pillow because of the vertigo. For the next three days I continued feeling dizzy and was aware of a high-pitched noise.

At the time I hadn't a clue as to how to interpret the dream. I didn't know my doctor well nor understand what my subconscious association with him was about. However, he and Elizabeth were the only key players in the dream whom I knew in the waking. They might hold a key to the dream's message. What I didn't want to accept, however, was that my friend would react negatively to the dream. Ignoring the warning, I called Elizabeth in California and recounted as much of what had become a nightmare as seemed relevant. She said the dream accurately described her feelings. Aliens, if they existed, had no correspondence to her spiritual path nor any other aspect of life.

Despite feeling alarmed by her reaction, as predicted in the dream, I understood her perspective. If the UFO and alien symbolism had not been recurring in my interior life, I might have reacted similarly. But as they were, I was still deep into a paradigm I didn't understand. All I knew for certain was that my dream reflected something that was happening to me. Because the feelings of being under 'the influence' of a force outside myself were so strong, I knew it was important to consciously understand the content. Whether the feelings emanated from my unconscious or from elsewhere, I wanted to know their source.

I thought about telling Dr West about his part in the dream, but was concerned that he would be put off, as Elizabeth had been, making for a strained relationship. I wanted to continue receiving his services on good terms through the duration of vog.

James West had the air of a seagoer as he stood tall and strong, with curly black hair and a swarthy Mediterranean complexion. There was humor in his dove-colored eyes as he joked and bantered, but at times they assumed a far-seeing gaze that intensified their mystic gray.

I was pleased when, after several visits, he dropped his professional reserve, and became more informal. I bided my time and looked for

Volcanic Visions

clues as to how well he would receive my dream until one day Dr West opened the door for me. He told me his son, David, who was around the same age as Josh, was visiting from Malta, where he lived with his mother and sister. James wanted to know if I would like for us all to get together. 'Yes,' I said.

11

WALKING ON COALS

Kalapana

*Turquoise waters beat
against jagged black rocks.*

*Children laugh
in the foaming surf
while breathing sulfur
from a burning mountain.*

*Sunbathers soak
on the black sand beach
as seaspray licks down
beads of sweat*

*knowing at any moment
we could be consumed
by the lavascape.*

I lay on the black sand beach writing poetry while Josh and David went boogie-boarding in the surf. I felt more and more sensual as I watched the foaming sea and brief raindrops sprinkled on my back, cooling the Hawaiian sun. I looked around at the heavy, drooping coconuts on the palms, very ripe and ready to roll on the beach and looked at the tan, muscular Hawaiian men and felt an erotic desire that continued to sweep over me like the waves on the beach. When a couple of the men made advances toward me, I tried to turn off the poetic juices and lay inert, like a seashell on the shore.

Late in the afternoon, when James was home from work, I brought David back and stayed for dinner. While James was busy making after-dinner cappuccinos, I decided that the time had come to talk about the extraterrestrial dream. I sipped the frothed milk off the hot coffee, and coyly said, 'James, I had a dream about you.'

'And . . .?' he said.

'I'm sure you'll laugh. In the dream I had a neckpiece with the face of an extraterrestrial on it. It was *your* face! With the neckpiece I could call down a Mother Ship.' I proceeded to tell him all the details. To my surprise, he didn't make a joke or ridicule me, but listened with intense seriousness. 'What is it, James?' I asked. 'Why so serious?'

'There's a lot I haven't told you, Michele. For the last few months, since you've been coming to me, I've been fighting the experience of falling into trances. I'd like to explore the phenomenon more, but it makes it difficult for me to stay focused at work.' I started to speak, but he went on.

'This isn't the first time that I've had spontaneous altered states. About twelve years ago I was living with my ex-wife on Malta. We were both involved with a Sufi group and experienced intense psychic phenomena due to our spiritual meditative practices and the powerful spiritual energy of our group and leader. I was traveling out of body and was so sensitive to other people's thoughts, I began isolating myself to try to shut down my wide-open clairvoyance. I felt very vulnerable and decided to find a way to stay grounded. I began to study aikido, and eventually became grounded again.

'Several years later I was with a woman friend on a hike and we noticed a glowing ball of orange light coming from a tree. Upon examination it appeared as an orange flame and we experienced a strange sensory perception.

'Then I moved to this island and have been doing well in my medical practice, staying mainstream. I've pretty much avoided anything esoteric since my move to the Big Island until you came along. And now here I am with you, feeling very open again.'

As I sat listening to him, I suddenly noticed that the redwood walls of his home were like those of the house in my dream. Also, I was experiencing intense pressure in my third eye and a feeling of vertigo when I was with him. I told James that there were an increasing number of elements relating him to the dream I had. I questioned what it meant or where it was leading. 'We'll probably understand it soon, Michele,' was all he said.

Walking on Coals

A few days later Josh and I met James and David to go swimming in the river. In order to get there we had to go through a jungle of trees and bushes. Clad in bathing suits, with thong sandals on our feet, we pushed our way through scratching branches and thick undergrowth until we came to the river. It was swollen, swirling down into rapids and swept into waterfalls. Looking at the turbulence, I thought it was crazy to go swimming, dangerous for the inexperienced even to enter a river in this state.

Before I could speak, James and the boys had jumped into the river. They appeared at ease in the aggressive water, and Josh was agilely picking his way around rocks, swimming downstream without getting swept away. I cautiously slipped into the swirling water. From the start I had a terrible time, slipping over rocks and having difficulty finding the bottom of the river with my feet. When we came close to the rapids I yelled to Josh to get out of the river, but saw that he had already reached less turbulent waters. Even though he had skilfully made his way, I thought perhaps I was mad to have proceeded with this adventure.

As I sat on a rock and considered how to get myself to the next less turbulent stretch of river without being swept over a waterfall, I thought about the last remotely similar experience Josh and I had shared. It had occurred the year before. Larissa Vilenskaya, whom I had profiled in *Shape Shifters*, was organizing a firewalking ceremony and wanted me to write an article on it for the *Psi Research Journal*, of which she was the publisher. I had taken Josh with me because I didn't have childcare for him and thought he would find the experience interesting.

In an upstairs room in a geodesic house we listened to a two-hour explanation of the mechanics of firewalking and a discussion about the empowerment that could be achieved by overcoming fear and resistance to 'walking'. We learned a song, which we repeated many times until it became a chant: 'Release your mind. See what you'll find. Bring it on home to your people.'

Suddenly, Josh, who had been unusually still during the discussion, got up quietly and looked over the balcony. He whispered for me to join him. Together we looked down at the fire blazing in the fire pit below. In a soft voice Josh said, 'You're not going to "walk", are you, Mom!?'

Volcanic Visions

I laughed. 'No way, Josh. Are *you*?' I asked teasingly.

'*No way!*' he almost shouted.

We rejoined the group, and heard a few people who had 'walked' previously testify how it had changed their lives. I listened with interest, but found them curiously like religious transformational testimonies I had heard. We began to chant again, and were reminiscent of a monastic procession as we filed down the stairs into the darkness outside: 'Release your mind. See what you'll find. Bring it on home to your people.' As we assembled around the pit I was relieved to see that the fire had become glowing red embers on the charcoal briquets.

The chanting continued softly. Larissa stepped on to the coals. She held her head up and walked at a regular pace across the pit. Next, a man stepped out and, with much bravado, walked at a fast pace over the coals. On the other side someone squirted his feet with a garden hose, as there was an ember caught between his toes.

I heard the sound of crying in the darkness. 'I want to "walk",' a young woman told Larissa through her tears. 'I think I would become so much stronger. But I'm afraid.' To measure her worth by whether or not she could firewalk seemed to me strange, but I realized the extent to which we all pit ourselves against a 'norm' and socially designated rites of passage.

Josh walked up to me and said in a quiet, clear voice, 'Mom, I want to walk.' I was thrown by his sudden desire to participate, but he seemed so calm and resolute that I decided to trust his capability and inner attunement. He walked unhurriedly across the 1200°F coals. On his face was a meditative look that reflected his practice of 'going within', which came from his training in the martial art of Sennin Do. When Josh returned to me on the other side of the fire pit, his face glowed serene and joyful. At home that evening he showed me a card that Larissa had given him, which said, 'Now you can do anything.'

Today he was swimming through rapids and waterfalls. James came up to me beside the rock, and asked, 'Are you going to leave your perch?' I nodded and slipped back into the water. He guided me through the least turbulent course as we wended our way along the 'boiling pots'. I slipped on the rocks a few times and my knees were bleeding from the cuts.

James told me that the kids had gone ahead to a place called the Emerald Pool. When we came to where they were playing, I sucked in my breath. A palpable presence in the place remained undisturbed, even with two boisterous children diving and splashing under the waterfall. Cumulus clouds, rocks and trees were mirrored in the emerald pool, colored by the lush green foliage surrounding it. Elemental spirits were invisibly present in the jade circle.

James got out of the water and sat on a volcanic rock overlooking the pool. The sensual smile on his lips said that he relished every aspect of being in the mandala. I lingered in the water, holding on to a rock. From the solid grounding, I stared into the blueness above watching the life force surging through the clouds. The atmosphere was pulsating and my motionless hands clutching the rock were filled with the etheric bioplasm. James lay on his rock and occasionally looked over, subtly watching. I smiled at him, glad to be friends yet have psychic space. I let go of the rock and dived deeply into the verdant pool.

That night I dreamt I flew over rocks and streams until I came to a hermitage in the mountains. There I saw my astral lover before a fireplace. He was shaping a piece of paper into an intentional form. Then he threw the paper into the fire and said, 'I will not give up on her, but will draw her to me.'

'I am here,' I said, and tried to push through the astral veil to join him in the flesh. I awakened with my covers on the floor. The air was filled with the torpid scent of sulfur and the heaviness of vog. Pele was burning.

12

VOLCANIC SEEDS

Smoking woman
spewing into the atmosphere
sulphurous dreams
of a god man
in the flesh

Ryan called to tell me that he had been soaking in the hot tub the night before when he saw a flash of light streaking through the darkness. More brilliant than a falling star, the object landed somewhere on the outskirts of Hilo. I looked in the paper* and noted that the sighting had been reported. There was speculation as to whether the light had been caused by space debris burning up as it fell through the atmosphere, or by some unknown object. An ad on the same page offered a reward to anyone who might have located remnants of the fallen object.

I called the man who had placed the ad. He told me that no one had reported any finds yet, but he was hopeful that remnants would be recovered. Dan, it turned out, was a mineralogist and Hawaiian mythology specialist. He had explored a lot of the island and, with a couple of friends, had discovered a site known as Kapo Cave. When they publicized their find, the Hawaiian community became concerned because the cave was sacred ground formerly used for rituals and as a burial chamber for Hawaiian royalty. Following a request from the islanders, the cave was to be sealed off.

'The historic tube is believed to contain several burial tombs and religious chambers with the remains of over one hundred persons, including Hawaiian royalty,' the newspaper had reported. Because

---

* *Hilo Tribune Herald*, July 30, 1987.

the cave has a characteristic genitalia formation, experts believe it is the birthplace of the legend of Kopokohelele (Kapo of the flying vagina), which tells how Pele's sister, the goddess Kapo, lured the fertility god, Kamapua'a, away from Pele to save her from his lurid intentions.

According to the legend, Kamapua'a desired Pele the first time he glimpsed her with her sister Kapo, and immediately devised plans to conquer her. Kapo, a psychic and sorcerer, apprehended Kamapua'a's intent and conjured up an illusion to divert his attention while Pele got away. As Kamapua'a chased a flying sexual organ that he thought belonged to the volcano goddess, Kapo and Pele howled with hilarity and ran back to their smoking house in Puna.

Kamapua'a, the spirit of the rain and growing things, resided in Oahu as a resident chief. Ordinarily, the fertility god appeared to his clan as an endearing, strikingly handsome man, but when his shadow side took over, he became an overbearing, lecherous animal. As a shape shifter, or *kapua*, he alternated between the form of a man, a hog and a fish.

Thinking about Pele one day, he was consumed with desire for her and with rage that she had eluded him. Undaunted by his own foolish actions and the failure of his first attempt, Kamapua'a vowed to satisfy his lust for her. He prepared his magic arts to assist him in conquering the goddess of fire, and set off for Puna in a boat, wearing a long black cape to hide the short bristles on his back. He crossed the two hundred miles of the Pacific that separated them, until he arrived at the southeastern point of Hawaii, where he moored his boat along the edge of the black sands. Walking the many miles to Kilauea, Kamapua'a followed the smoke that was spewing out of the black cinder cone. When he arrived at last at the growing mountain, he climbed the smoking vent to the top and peered down into the blazing chambers of Pele's home.

Smoke swirled around Kamapua'a's head as he strained to see the fire dance that was taking place in the bowels of the Earth. Through the filmy light he could just make out the silhouettes of Pele and her sisters as they danced with undulating movements over the top of the seething magma. Like wraiths, they moved with sinuous gestures, their arms, legs and hips telling the volcano's story. In the magic of the hula their diaphanous dresses reflected the crimson of the fire and the blue haze of the smoke, and were blown about with gusts from exploding bubbles around them.

Suddenly, the smoke shifted direction and the veil through which Kamapua'a was gazing lifted. The dancing fire deities gasped when they looked up and saw a stranger witnessing their sacred ritual. When one of the sisters met Kamapua'a's gaze, however, she was touched by desire for the muscular, intense man. She called out to Pele, 'Oh, my sister, you must lift your taboo so that I can have this man!' But Pele was not impressed. She recognized the man who had pursued her, the sorcerer whom she and Kapo had tricked. She had shunned his advances the first time and knew that he had come for her again. Kapo was not at home to aid her, so Pele had to use her own resources to repel the *kapua*.

She launched a vicious verbal onslaught, certain that he would reveal his true nature in return. After Pele had called him every pig and hog insult that her imagination could devise, Kamapua'a responded as she had expected. He began hurling equally offensive insults at the powerful volcano goddess, to which she then retaliated by raising a shower of hot lava out of the cinder cone to destroy the boorish *kapua*.

Exercising his magical energy, Kamapua'a ran at lightning speed to the sea, where he transformed into a spiny fish and swam away from the fury of Pele. She chased him with burning pillows of underwater magma, but Kamapua'a was protected by his rough exterior and skillfully eluded the boiling lava. Convinced that she had permanently quelled Kamapua'a's lust for her, Pele went home and rejoined her sisters and brothers in their fire temple.

Like a hunter rejoicing in the challenge of a difficult prey, Kamapua'a returned to Pele's sanctuary. But she heard him outside stealthily climbing her mountain and responded with blasts of fire and rocks. His adrenalin aroused for the fight, Kamapua'a immediately called down torrential rains to put out her flames. The elements of fire and water battled back and forth, but after a while it became apparent that the rains were dampening the volcanic fire. Pele's brothers were the keepers of the flames, the holders of the magic fire sticks that kept their home heated. If the fire went out, the volcanic family would perish. With great reluctance, the brothers implored Pele to submit to Kamapua'a's desires.

Revolted as she was at the thought, Pele knew that she had little choice but to consent to Kamapua'a's wishes. As she tried to prepare herself mentally as a sacrifice to save her family Pele came to a startling realization: on a physical level she was attracted to this exotic man and wanted him, as he did her. At the same time she knew she would not allow Kamapua'a to dominate her.

Pele and Kamapua'a's marriage was a union of two warring demi-gods. Although Kamapua'a was her fourth husband, and the one she loved the least, he was the one with whom Pele created the most new acreage for the island. They made passionate, wild love, fertilizing the lava with their mana, planting volcanic seeds, but in their day-to-day relationship they had irreconcilable differences. Pele loved and needed the hot, dry smoke lodge for her well-being; Kamapua'a longed for the lush rain forest along the Hamakua coast, where he rooted for moist growing things. He was affectionate when appeased, but ruthless when denied any pleasure. She was volatile, exploding at little provocation, and resisted yielding to many of her mate's wishes, in fear of his domination.

The warring lovers eventually agreed to live apart – Pele in the hot, volcanic districts that were her domain, and Kamapua'a in the wet, verdant terrain that was his kingdom – except for brief interludes, when they would meet to renew their passion, and the fertile lushness of the islands.

I entered the depths of Kapo Cave in imagination, but because it was *kapu*, a secret place, taboo to outsiders, I didn't seek to enter it physically. Returning to the reason for my call, I asked Dan to let me know when he learned more about the object that had dropped from the sky.

13

NUMINOUS PLACES

> *Kamapua'a's spirit
> in pregnant gray clouds
> shakes a blessing rain
> with pulsating power
> on those born again
> in the* heiau
> *place of refuge*

The Harmonic Convergence was to be celebrated as a sacred sites festival around the world, at which people would gather together to generate and project thoughts of world peace. It was hoped that the astronomical alignment, combined with collective meditation, would create positive long-term planetary transformation. It was also prophesied that a spiritual quickening would occur in the hearts of many people at that time, initiating new spiritual leaders and healers who would be needed during the global cleansing and transition that would precede the planetary shift into the fifth world.

Two festivals were being planned on the Big Island. At Halemaumau, a *kahuna* was preparing an all-night ritual to bring balance between the island community and the goddess Pele. According to many followers of the Huna religion, the invasive geothermal work being conducted by the government was responsible for the volcanic activity that had been going on since 1983, which had made many people ill with upper-respiratory infections. The *kahuna* selected the Harmonic Convergence as the right time for the healing ritual to take place.

At the *kahuna*'s house a group of people were selecting chants, songs and offerings for the matriarch of the volcano. As I listened to their plans I felt detached from the process, and realized that attune-

Numinous Places

ment to the volcano's mysteries had become a private experience. Every morning and evening I communed with the deity of the island, who in some archetypal way is part of the female psyche, like the shadow, the dark side of the moon. By focusing on the volcanic forces within me, I was facing my own demons, as well as my own savior, a transformational power.

Pele, like Persephone and Hecate, personifies the inner terrain, the unconscious, with all its power, potential and shadow side. In their raw forms the forces from this terrain are destructive and devouring, portrayed archetypically by the 'terrible mother'. When they are worked with and integrated, these same forces are transforming energies that bring about transmutation, rebirth and enlightenment.

Staring into Halemaumau, the yawning black crater of Kilauea, the primal fears of the dark side of the mother were awakened. In *The Great Mother* Erich Neumann says, 'The gate, door, gully, ravine, abyss are symbols of the feminine earth-womb, they are the numinous places that mark the road into the mythical darkness of the underworld.'* I felt consumed by the terrible unknown power in myself, which has the potential to devour physically and psychically, and yet is a shamanic place, the underworld. By journeying into the depths of the fear, facing the demon–deity who lives there, the core of being is revealed, along with the face of death. Facing the shadow of death is the turning point where true power becomes accessible and transformation begins.

The mysteries of Pele were working silently within me, in the womb, the tomb, the tantric stirrings of myself. However, there are five volcanoes on the island and it was not to Kilauea and its Halemaumau crater I was called that night. Something behind the scenes was drawing me elsewhere on August 16.

I learned that plans were also being made for the Kona side of the island at a site called Kilohana, which means 'Stargazer'. At Kilohana, the place where three volcanoes meet and form a triangle, I was told that UFOs have been sighted for no one knows how long.

---

*Erich Neumann, *The Great Mother*, Princeton, NJ, Princeton University Press, 1974, p. 170.

Volcanic Visions

Some of the people organizing the festival believed the old Meso-American prophecies indicated that the extraterrestrials would be making contact with people at designated power spots around the globe at this time to prepare them for the movement of the planet into the fifth world. There was speculation that Kilohana might be one of those sites.

I didn't believe that extraterrestrials had an appointed date with humanity on one cosmic night according to an interpretation of ancient prophecies. I did, however, have a fascination with a place whose name means Stargazer.

James and I were discussing doing something significant together. He suggested we climb Mauna Loa, and I mentioned the Harmonic Convergence celebrations. He hadn't heard anything about them at that point, so I shared what I knew. I withheld telling him my preference, because I was curious about which site he would gravitate to. When I finished, James was looking pensive. After a long silence, he said to me, with conviction, 'We're going to Kilohana – to make contact.'

I looked at him quickly to see if he was kidding, but he had the same trance-like expression as when I told him about the dream of the ET neckpiece with his face on it. I studied his deep gray eyes and wondered.

Two nights before the Convergence, James called. There was an odd quality to his voice. 'Shall we go with "them"?'

I knew what he was implying, but regardless of my 'paranormal' experiences, there was a line of credulity I didn't want to cross. I was concerned about the degree to which he was leaving behind boundaries. My response was caustic. 'You mean, what will "you" do if "they" come?'

'We both need to make a commitment and be sure our kids are with us,' he said.

I considered calling off the whole excursion, but was torn, because I had wanted to go with James and to explore the area surrounding Kilohana.

Before we ended our strange conversation, James said, 'Please promise me that you'll ask Josh if he wants to come with us.'

'OK,' I said to humor him. Inwardly I was having trouble

connecting this James with the pleasant, down-to-earth doctor I had been seeing.

As I was tucking my son into bed I remembered James's request and thought Josh would have a good laugh. 'James wanted you to come with us and be company for David. But I told him that you already have plans – you're going to the baseball All-Star picnic.'

'You've got that right!' he said. 'We're going to spend the whole day swimming, barbecuing, and playing baseball at the beach.'

'Sounds great! We're mostly going to play music, sing and meditate. And they say there are a lot of UFO sightings around there. That could be interesting.'

'Sounds boring.'

In jest, I said, 'It might be. Unless a UFO comes by and offers us a ride.'

Josh looked stricken. 'Mom, you wouldn't go, would you?'

I was startled by how seriously he took it. 'No, of course not,' I said.

14

CONVERGENCE

Mauna Kea

*If the mountain is our meeting place
I must be there by summer
before the mountain blows
or before our memories drift on
to another lifetime.*

*Our ancient vows linger
like clouds hovering
above the volcanic slopes
where our reunion is held
— suspended.*

August 16 was a beautiful day in Hilo, with no vog in the sky. The volcanic haze was blowing Kona-side and there was no sign of rain. Midafternoon I drove to Richardson's beach, where Josh met his baseball team, and then I headed out to Keaau, to James's house. On the way I had some anxious thoughts about him, but brushed them aside. It occurred to me he might have been kidding all along about his preoccupation with meeting ETs. I didn't know him well enough to be certain.

James complimented me on my red Balinese dress with dragon motif, worn for celebration, but it was thin and he was concerned I'd freeze where we were going. Being new to the islands, it was easy for me to underestimate how cold it gets in the volcanic mountains. The only thing that put a slight damper on the mood was that James made an issue out of Josh not being there, as if our plans would be foiled. But then he dropped it and turned his attention to last-minute preparations.

Just as I was ready to zip home and do a quick change James's

Convergence

physician buddy, Glenn, pulled up in his baby Mercedes. He was anxious to leave right away, as he was meeting his woman friend in Kilohana, so James disappeared into his room for a few minutes and came out holding a set of clothes. 'For me?' I asked incredulously. We all burst out laughing, as James is over six feet tall, and I'm only five foot three.

In a good humor, the four of us got the sleeves and cuffs rolled up, and James found a huge belt to hold up the pants. A big bulky sweater helped hide the workings of the assemblage. I was so out of character, and felt so silly and childlike dressed in a big man's clothes, that I was ready for anything.

We were all very lighthearted and sang songs as we rolled along in James's jeep. He drove at a fast clip along the Saddle Road, which was the rough but quick way to Kilohana, on the other side of the island. As we left Hilo behind, we entered volcanic terrain. Shrubby oh'ia trees stuck out of ancient lava flows from extinct Mauna Kea, towering ahead of us. We all became more serious when we approached the volcano. Suddenly, the huge giant disappeared into dense fog and oh'ia trees appeared out of the filmy mass like wraiths. James had to slow down to a crawl. I was surprised that the fog was so thick there; the sea and active volcano were miles away. I looked over at James and saw his jaw tighten. He stared out with a strange expression. I immediately felt uncomfortable.

'I've never seen it look like this before,' he said.

'What do you mean?' I asked.

'I've never seen Mauna Kea enshrouded with so much fog.' He strained his eyes to see the road. 'They're up there,' he said.

'Oh Goddess, here we go,' I thought.

'Who's up there, Dad?' David called out from the back seat.

'We'll see,' was all James would say.

I stared at the thick fog rolling in, very glad that I wasn't doing the driving this time. James and Glenn talked about their practices, and about friends I didn't know. Glenn was in the back seat with David, and had to talk over my back. My attention was on James, the strange look in his eyes and the thick fog. I hoped the fog would go away, I really hoped it would go away. It was going to be a long day and night. Finally, we passed the long flanks of Mauna Kea and the fog lifted.

Volcanic Visions

'We're going up there,' I heard James mutter under his breath. 'OK, everybody, we'll be in Kilohana in twenty minutes,' he said out loud.

'Yeah!' David cheered from the back.

Relieved to be out of the cold heaviness of the fog we began to revive as we drove along stretches of grassy meadows, three volcanoes looming ahead. The sun was full and warming. James pulled up to a wooden gate that said 'Kilohana Girl Scout Camp'.

'Girl Scout Camp!' yelled David, in a deprecating voice.

'Don't worry,' said his dad, laughing. 'The troops won't be here today!' As we pulled into the parking lot I suddenly became self-conscious about the ridiculous get-up I had on, but then became distracted by the scene. Krishna devotees chanted and played on *kurtals* (brass cymbals) and drums in the parking lot. Numerous tents were pitched in the outer area of the camp, and children and dogs ran through the grass between them. At water spigots around the area women and men in jeans and rainbow-colored shirts were rinsing off remnants of lunch from tin pans. Most of the people had set up house in the camp the day before and were relaxing before the evening celebration.

We strolled over to the central gathering area with its empty stage; it was about an hour before the scheduled live music. A few folks were strumming guitars by an open fire pit, where a couple of people were barbecuing. People gradually began to congregate near the stage. James and Glenn mingled, introducing me to many friends and clients. Then Bobbi, Glenn's woman friend, showed up wearing designer clothes. I tried to forget the makeshift outfit I was wearing.

Around 6:30 or 7 o'clock a rock and roll band set up their equipment and began to wail. No one we had heard of, or liked. As the music got louder, James whispered to me that it was time to go. David overheard him and was immediately ready to depart. James went over to Bobbi and Glenn. 'Let's go.'

'Where? We've come all this way!' Glenn exclaimed.

'Come on. I'll tell you in the jeep.'

Back on the road again we were all a little unsettled. We had been prepared for a group celebration, but instead we were heading

Convergence

for one of the most remote parts of the island, Mauna Kea. However, Bobbi and Glenn in the back seat were amiable and soon relaxed – but David startled me when he called out, 'I know they're up there too, Dad.'

As we drove along, the sun sank fast and we re-entered the fog embankment. James drove much faster than he should have with so little visibility. He continued to drive swiftly around the narrow bends as we began to ascend the steep mountain. The couple in the back seat remained passive, but I was scared and my stomach was churning.

'Slow down, James.'

He slowed down somewhat but his face had a 'driven' expression. 'We've got to get up there,' was all he said.

'Hello – James!' I tried to bring him to attention, to snap him out of it, but he didn't respond. It occurred to me that he had seen *Close Encounters* one too many times.

I looked out to see if there was any semblance of view left, but it was too dark. We were above the fog, however. James pulled into the Onizuku Visitor Center, a midway point to the top of Mauna Kea. On Saturday evenings professional and amateur astronomers brought small telescopes to the parking lot for star gazing, but on this Sunday night only one person was there with a telescope set up.

We piled out of the jeep and looked up at the night sky, the Milky Way expansive and filmy white. A light moved across the expanse in a downward motion. James said it was a satellite circling the Earth, seen only at great altitudes. We craned our necks, identifying planets and constellations.

The man with the telescope called out for us to see something he was viewing. James looked first, letting out a low whistle. He was followed by the others, who each let out some kind of exclamation. I stood back staring up at the Milky Way spread across the sky, with a dense filminess I had never seen at lower altitudes. Then I took my turn to look into the telescope. I thrilled at a white ringed ball glowing in perfect symmetry against the black backdrop of space. The beauty of Saturn was all the more pristine seen through this porthole in the sky.

I wondered who this stranger in the dark was, who offered a window into the universe. When I asked his name, I was surprised at his answer. 'We spoke when I called the observatory to request a press pass to see Prince Philip,' I said. 'You made the arrangements with the BBC.'

'That's right.'

'By the way, thanks! You weren't there when I phoned to tell you what a success it was.'

He laughed. 'And we meet face to face – star gazing.'

James was anxious to continue our journey. 'It's not far to the top. Let's get going.'

The astronomer overheard. 'It's better you don't. They are working late in the observatory tonight and would rather not have any car lights or any distractions.'

We agreed, saying goodnight and thanking him for the view of Saturn. We piled into the jeep, and James proceeded up the mountain. 'What are you doing?' I asked. 'He told us not to go up.'

'We're going to the top,' is all he would say. For the time we were at Onizuku I had forgotten about this 'other James'. But it was he who drove on to an area off limits.

When we arrived, I took a deep breath. Appearing very different at night, the several white observatories were spread across the moon-lit landscape in surreal contrast to the darkness. They stood like sentinels at the top of the world, silent confirmation of the sci-fi-like reality. As we faced its titanic shell, the Mauna Kea Observatory made a slow whine, opening as it shifted on its axis, facing the edge of the cliff. We sat in the car expectantly, as if we were in the opening scene of Arthur C. Clarke's *2010*. The open dome, housing the infrared telescope stood directly in front of us, glowing in the starlight.

We thrilled when we stepped out of the car into the virgin silence, like astronauts stepping out on lunar soil. The air was frigid at 13,000 feet above sea level. Wrapped in heavy jackets, we hugged ourselves in exhilaration, the rarefied air going straight to our heads. Sparkling sapphires, rubies and diamonds hung from varying depths in black space. Gone were the flat skies seen at lower altitudes. Our minds were filled with stars and heavenly bodies, with teeth chattering, we were high on space.

His voice sober again, James said, 'Let's put our minds together and call down a Mother Ship.' He borrowed the idea from my dream about the neckpiece with his face on it. But out of ritualized respect for the cosmos, which I felt so close to, I visualized our group thought-form like a communiqué reaching an extraterrestrial intelligence. There were a few moments of silence in which we all at least pretended to send a cosmic message.

Then we returned to our own reveries, in which walking on top of the world was so profound, so cold and as exquisite an experience. James looked enraptured and wonderful, the tension erased. Then, in a quiet, weighty voice he said softly, 'Look at the lights.' I heard the innuendo and wanted to ignore it. Then only a little louder, as if spotting a wild animal, not wanting to frighten it, he said again, 'Look at the lights.'

Glancing over to where he was pointing, I saw two huge amber headbeams that seemed to be coming our way. I assumed that they were from an oversized truck on the windy road. 'No large truck can get up this road,' he said softly. 'Besides those lights aren't coming from the road. We're facing the cliff.'

In the dark it was very hard for me to orient myself spatially. But I tried to review how we were situated. On one side was the road, but our car was parked about fifty yards away from, and facing, the cliff, as the Mauna Kea Observatory was also situated between the cliff and road.

Glenn and Bobbi let out several exclamations. I was startled and turned around to face the lights appearing and disappearing mysteriously. I couldn't suspend my disbelief. 'It's a car coming up the road. We're seeing the lights each time it comes around a bend.'

'Michele, if the lights were coming from the road, the vehicle would have arrived by now.' With a steady voice, he continued, 'The lights are coming from the cloud.'

Even seeing the cloud, I had trouble accepting it.

'Let's drive down to the spot where I think the lights are coming from.' We followed James into the jeep and drove half a mile down the road. James stopped, turning off the lights.

As we sat in the darkness I felt my defenses surface. 'How long do you want to sit here?' No one answered. Then, from out of a cloud two amber lights appeared. This time I couldn't dispute that we were facing the cliff's edge.

Out of slight hysteria, I began to giggle. Trying to approach it rationally, 'What kind of flying object has two amber lights?' As a group they hushed me. I was annoyed, but also vaguely aware that my reaction to the whole experience wasn't congruent with my earlier quest. I had been enthralled by the vision of a UFO and intrigued by the channeled reading in which I was told I would see a Mother Ship. Yet having a sighting of some kind, I was unnerved, mostly because it all seemed to be going according to a plan. The sighting was foretold and James had been acting as if from a script. But denial and indifference evaporated.

Suddenly the headbeams rose up from out of the cloud and an enormous wheel of rotating lights appeared, flickering like a giant spinning sparkler. There was a magical quality to the dazzling wheel, like fairy lights. 'Oh God!' I cried out, while everyone else had responses of awe. We were all on the edge of our seats peering out, the brilliant flying object reminiscent of the flying ship of a vision, shimmering against the black volcanic mountain. I felt a tingling shoot through my body, transmitted perhaps from the space vehicle. I had no doubt the Mother Ship had come.

As we sat there in rapture, a suspended, altered state, the lights disappeared again behind the cloud, and James broke the mood. 'Let's go back down to Kilohana. They may be taking people aboard.'

That didn't make sense to me. We had just been viewing the UFO on the top of Mauna Kea. Why would he want to leave now? There was no telling what we might have seen next had we waited. And if we had gotten out of the jeep . . .

But James started up the motor. In the back seat Glenn, Bobbi and David were as passive as they had been all night. No one protested but me, and I did so silently. Why didn't I tell him to wait a few minutes? Everything had led up to this moment. James had brought us here. He had said, 'I want to go with them.' Why, then, was he ruining his chances by leaving the mountaintop when maybe 'they' were still up there hidden in a cloud? Somewhat shaken and confused, I swallowed my objections and let him take control. I felt I was being manipulated by unseen forces and hoped I was being led to something significant.

Still looking driven, James sped down the steep mountain road. Halfway down, we re-entered dense fog, but James never slowed his frantic pace. We arrived at the camp at 11:30. Most of the people had already settled in their tents, but a small group was still assembled around the campfire. Their faces looked listless. We agreed amongst ourselves not to tell anyone at the camp that we had seen a UFO, since they had all assembled at Kilohana for that purpose and were disappointed by the 'no show'.

As we left, James drove more slowly in the direction of Hilo. Somewhere beyond Kilohana he pulled into an area off the road where the fog was particularly turbid. I was astounded when Bobbi got out of the jeep and walked over to a car that was barely visible in the mist. Hers was the only car there. She got in and waved goodbye to us.

'Is it safe for her to drive alone out here, in this fog?' I asked.

'Sure,' both James and Glenn replied.

And why, I thought, was she parked way out here, far from the camp parking lot? But I kept silent. Things had stopped making sense.

James drove on, then made another stop in the fog. He turned out his lights and waited. Nothing happened. He got out of the jeep, walked up the road, came back and turned on the motor again. We were all silent.

As we got closer to Hilo, I felt the energy shift in the car. James looked as though he was regrouping, and Glenn sat back and relaxed. With a return to some normality, I lightened up and wanted to talk about the phenomenon on Mauna Kea. 'You knew all along we were going to see a UFO!' I said to James. 'That's extraordinary!'

He had again become the self-possessed person I knew, only now he was more reserved than usual. 'I'm sure there's an explanation for what we saw,' he said.

'That's right,' said Glenn.

'What?!' I asked.

'I just think that what we saw didn't appear out of nowhere,' James replied. 'Maybe it was a military operation. Besides, I'm tired and don't want to talk about it any more tonight.'

I was incredulous. After all that, and now he was in denial.

David spoke up loudly from the back seat. 'You can't fool me. You know we saw a UFO.'

James and Glenn began to talk about a medical conference coming

Volcanic Visions

up. I sank back in my seat. I wanted us to share our experience, but would have to, it seemed, process my experience alone. Perhaps validating it within myself was part of the initiation.

When we got back to James's house, he said I was welcome to stay the night, but I felt I couldn't get home too soon. My knees were weak as I drove back to Hilo. Before going to sleep, however, I thrilled to the thought of the two headbeams rising out of the cloud, with the enormous spinning wheel of lights below.

The next morning, on Monday, I called the army base. I asked if they had had any air vehicles up over Mauna Kea the night before. The officer manning the phones told me, 'They were hot last night. The army fired explosives, and other ground military operations were going on, but nothing in the air.'

I described what we had seen. 'In all honesty,' he said, 'we do see things out there that we don't have any explanation for. I don't know what it was you saw.'

I talked to James on the phone. He sounded 'back to normal' but still didn't want to talk about the experience at Mauna Kea. I spent the rest of the day lying in the sun on the beach, mulling over the events that had taken place the night before. I realized that the army officer could have been lying about having no air vehicles up at the time of our sighting. It was conceivable that the military had created an enormous aerial craft for covert military operations and was experimenting with it on the mountain.

I still had many unanswered questions, such as why James seemed 'called' to the volcano and, while exhibiting erratic behavior, 'knew' we were going to see a 'ship'. It was uncanny as well that putting our minds together to contact a UFO seemed to coincide with its appearance. I was reminded again of the dream in which I held a neckpiece with James's face on it and used it like a radar signal to call down a Mother Ship. The appearance was also similar to the vision I had in which I saw a luminous space ship against the backdrop of a dark volcanic mountain. In both instances the lights triggered the feeling of an electrical shock transmitted on a neurological level.

I wondered what the composite effect of the experience was on our whole group. It was possible that more transpired than we remembered, because we all seemed thrown by the experience. James, who had been led to the mountaintop, did not want to talk about the sighting. Bobbi was dropped off at a remote spot and never really voiced her feelings. Glenn, like James, dismissed the experience. David had remained receptive and enthusiastic throughout the adventure, and I, who have an interest in UFOs, was strangely unreceptive until contact, and then was somewhat disoriented by the appearance and felt as if I was in shock.

I thought it was also possible that we had had a chance meeting with an archetype through a series of synchronous events.

> A myth is essentially a product of the unconscious archetype and is therefore a symbol which requires psychological interpretation ... Should it be that an unknown physical phenomenon is the outward cause of the myth, this would detract nothing from the myth, for many myths have meteorological and other natural phenomena as accompanying causes which by no means explain them.*

If the meeting with the Mother Ship was a convergence with an archetype from our collective mythology, it was important to analyze what myth we were enacting.

The five of us who had been together at the sighting were all raised in the Judeo-Christian tradition, in which there is an expectation of a second coming of the Messiah. From beyond our three-dimensional world he will come, bringing light and the baptism of the holy spirit. According to the biblical prophecies, 'the anointed one' will vanquish the forces of evil and replace the old order of violence and confusion with peace and harmony. Similarly, the Hindu scriptures prophesy the return of Kalki; Buddhist prophecies anticipate the Maitreya, the Buddha of the future; and the worshipers of Gaia envision a rebirth and ascendance of the goddess. And so the collective mythology builds castles in the clouds, and we wait expectantly for the sacred messenger who will bring order out of chaos and provide answers where there appear to be none.

It is no wonder, then, that we are personally touched when a circular sphere appears out of the heavens, its mandala shape symbolizing

---

*C. G. Jung, *Flying Saucers: A Modern Myth of Things Seen in the Sky*, New York, Harcourt, Brace & Co., 1959, p. xii.

integration and unity.* Like a rotating *chakra*, the spinning wheel of supernatural light disseminates etheric energy. Powerful as lightning, the electromagnetic rays trigger *kundalini* activity, stimulating accelerated psychic development and spiritual aspiration. There is hope for ascension into heaven via the skyborn chariot, and a desire to return to a world of perfection and wholeness, the mythic plane of Po.

The messengers inside the ship are unknown agents, as if from God. Before they make themselves visible, they are beyond our conception, beyond our rational thought, and therefore are the agents of all possibility and potential. When 'touched' by the masters, the spiritual guardians of this or other worlds, we may 'wander in the desert' for a while, disoriented. Our world undergoes a change as we learn to respond to frequencies from higher and subtler dimensions. There is a transition from the known to the unknown, from one paradigm to another.

And somewhere in our memory is the 'face of God', the face of the ascended teacher, which was revealed to us in our own ascension. In the descent back to the world after 'going to the mountaintop' and seeing the face of God in the burning bush, reflected in a spinning disk, shimmering from behind a cloud, we know we are not the same; the transformation has begun.

For the masses, the UFO may symbolize unreality, fear of the unknown or the promise of another world, a new state of mind delivered by the long-awaited guardian or by the dove descending from a cloud. For the individual who has been touched by the symbol of the UFO, it triggers an awareness of the fourth dimension and beyond. I had had at least a fleeting contact with an extraterrestrial reality and believed the visitors to be the emissaries who came to me through the channeled reading. They had kept their promise: I had seen the Mother Ship. I knew it was they who had implanted the vision of the UFO in my consciousness.

I slept well after making contact with my own mythology, and felt protected by the guardians who hover so near the twilight and our world.

---

*ibid., p. 32.

15

THE DESCENT

Dreams stopped
as she flew past the moon
back
to
the
third
dimension

It had been a long time since I had heard African rhythms. In Kalapana the drum beat pulled me out of my head and into my body, swaying in syncopated movement like a palm. The dance troupe ignited the stage with passionate thrusts and perfect symmetry at Kalani Honua, the Cultural Arts Center. I moved across the grass feeling lightheaded, as if filled with strong wine, jungle cries on my lips. The Kalapana crowd danced in the spirit of the island, the performers on stage and on the grass a synergistic entity. Intoxicated by the ocean breeze and drums, I eventually fell to the ground and lay inhaling the earth and briny air.

When the drums eventually faded, I reluctantly rose and walked towards the pool where Josh had been playing with other kids for the last couple of hours. As I was leaving, I passed the lead male dancer, Eric, on the grass. 'Very fine. You are a powerful dancer,' I said. He started to move towards me, to talk more, but Josh said he wanted to go home. Because I was hesitant to initiate anything at that time, I said goodbye, feeling peevish as I drove past the phosphorescent sea, the magnetic pull of the moon arousing the waves. Filled with the evening music and the light of the moon, I wanted to throw my inhibitions and head away, like a coconut husk bobbing on the sea.

A visiting guru from Maui gave a *dharma* talk at the town center

Volcanic Visions

in Keaau. His words were inspiring, but I became distracted by another energy, another light across the room. It was Eric, the dancer from Kalapana. He sat in trance and I watched him, though he didn't see me. I delighted in seeing him again, and in that setting. However, I didn't feel brazen without the drums, and said nothing to him at the conclusion of the talk, but slipped away into the night.

I was becoming restless. My editor called several times from London to find out when I was going back to San Francisco to work on publicity for my first book, which was just coming out. I was still in the throes of my recent encounter on the mountain and needed to continue integrating the feelings. I tried talking about it with James, but he was closed to discussing the experience. I realized he probably was feeling uncomfortable and embarrassed about his erratic behavior and about losing some control to an outside force. But I still wanted to exchange thoughts and feelings with him, as no one in our party had been more deeply affected by the experience than he and I.

I talked to Ananda at length and was surprised by his receptivity and interest in our UFO experience. We spent a beautiful evening talking and chanting together. I told him Josh and I would be leaving the island soon, and we were both saddened about putting space and time between our friendship again.

For some reason, I dreaded telling James, but he had to know we were going at some point. So we got together to talk and it turned into a verbal joust.

'I can't believe you're doing this. Leaving in two weeks!'

'We had some interesting experiences together, which you don't want to talk about. Besides, we can meet again. You can visit us in California.'

'There could be something between us. You know that. You haven't given us time. There is so much about this island that you don't know. If you did, you wouldn't leave. Look – a short visit to California isn't enough. And I can never leave the island for long.'

'James, I have to get back to the mainland to work, to survive. And – the volcanic fumes are killing me.'

He couldn't argue with me on this last point. James was morose and so was I.

The Descent

I called Ryan to let him know we were leaving. He too seemed surprised. 'I could never leave this island,' he said. 'Once you know what this place is, you can't leave. I could be paid a salary many times over what I receive in Hilo, on Oahu or the mainland, but I can't leave. This is my home.'

'I understand. James said the same thing. But I guess my calling is different. I've got to get back to California.'

'You'll be back,' he said. 'I'm going to miss that son of yours too.' When I had brought Josh over to see Ryan's 'UFO' room, they had hit it off immediately. Ryan showed Josh many of his high-tech gadgets, and told him to raid the refrigerator so that we could feast while hanging out in the hot tub. Josh came back with huge sandwiches, sodas and bonbons, and wine for Ryan and me. We all had had a good time, and my feelings for Ryan mellowed considerably. Now he said he wanted to see us off at the airport; he would find time to get away from his lab to be there. I thanked him and couldn't help feeling I really didn't know my two friends, James and Ryan, very well.

After two weeks of getting ready, I was almost psyched up to go. James invited Josh and me over for a special dinner with him and David the night before we were to leave. James made a toast to our quick return to the island, but otherwise we talked very little. The boys finished dinner quickly and went upstairs to play.

I sipped my wine slowly and thought about all I had to do the next day to get ready for our departure. After several more minutes of silence, I got up to tell Josh that we had to leave. Suddenly the doorbell rang and a moment later we heard Josh cry out in pain.

I ran into the living room and found Josh crumpled up near the staircase, his face contorted, wailing something about his foot. I got down on the floor and examined his foot, which was rapidly swelling to what seemed like twice its normal size. I was vaguely aware of someone else kneeling next to me, expressing great concern.

'My God! What happened?' I asked.

'I don't know,' Josh said, still crying. 'The doorbell rang and we were going to answer it. But when I stepped down on the second step, my foot twisted.' He managed to get the words out, but was visibly in pain.

I got up, ready to rush Josh to the hospital emergency room.

Volcanic Visions

'He'll be alright – I can take care of him here,' James said.

'No – he's got to have the foot X-rayed,' I snapped.

Then the person who had just come in spoke. I looked up at him with more than surprise.

'Come on,' he said to me, taking my hand. 'We'll take Josh in my car.'

'OK, Eric,' I said. James and his friend carried Josh out to James's jeep, at his insistence.

At the hospital the guys wheeled him in for X-rays, which showed a fracture, and we left with Josh on crutches.

I took my traumatized son home to bed. The doctor had given him painkilling pills, and he was zonked out. I wondered how our trip would go. I suddenly felt very vulnerable and alone. How was I going to get about with Josh on crutches? How were we both going to adjust, moving back to a new place? With Josh's freakish accident, I almost felt there was some force trying to keep us there.

James called in the morning to see if we were going to cancel our trip. I told him resolutely, 'No.' A little while after Josh and I got to the airport with all our luggage Ryan, James and David showed up. The men had left work to see us off. They greeted us with presents. James put an orchid lei around my neck, repeating the folk saying, 'Unless you've been lei'ed in Hawaii, you won't return.' Ryan put a plumeria and orchid lei around my neck, and gave Josh a baseball mitt and a lot of sympathy for his foot.

The two kids looked awkward and upset about parting, and I again felt pangs about leaving. Ryan had to return to work but James stayed until our departure. He tried hard to get through to me at the last moment. 'We don't yet know what it's all about for us. It's too soon to leave.'

I knew I hadn't given us transition time. James had been behaving in ways even he didn't understand, and I assumed that eventually he would want to talk about it and analyze our experiences. It is possible that James and I were linked in a deeper way than I imagined, and had yet to pull aside the veil to know where we'd been. But I told myself that I had to be on familiar ground as I descended internally from our trip to Mauna Kea.

I heard the last call for our flight and hurried out the door while

The Descent

Josh limped along on his crutches. I turned around and called out 'Aloha!' James's last message still echoing in my ears: 'It's too soon to leave.'

Josh fell asleep soon after we boarded. He was still taking painkillers and was uncomfortable with the swollen, fractured foot. I nestled down in my seat, and during lift-off was most keenly aware of the scent of plumeria wafting up from the lei around my neck. The further we got from the islands, the more I felt a pulling and tearing inside.

Even though we were in the sky, I felt as though we were coming down. I was leaving behind friends and my relationship to the island itself. Had I stayed longer, I might have been drawn deeper into mythic Mu. Although his spiritual presence stayed with me, it seemed I also left behind some of my dreams of the man from the other side of the world, our trysts belonging to a lehua grove or the glowing trails of a burning mountain. Perhaps, like Pele, my soul would always wander, 'stirred by thoughts of faraway lands', until she came at last to the Big Island, creating a fire pit which she called home.

16

TWILIGHT

*Between worlds
the moon and the sun
appear as luminaries
in the same sky.
The outer and inner
become exchanged
inside out,
and uncertainty
becomes a constant.*

My move from Hawaii back to Marin County in northern California was more than a transition from one place to another: it was an abrupt change of climate and state of consciousness to a twilight place between two worlds. At first everything looked flat, the mana faint in the land from all the decades of pollution and neglect after the native guardians were slaughtered and the sacred rituals ignored. The people around me were living the great yuppie dream, and my friends were directed by a different compass than mine. Mine was attuned to Hilo, where east pointed to Mauna Loa, west to Hualalai, south to Kilauea and north to Mauna Kea. I had only one orientation in Marin, and that was to the 'sleeping lady' as she appears on Mount Tamalpais, the most dominant point of the skyline.

That was the despair I plunged into when I returned from Mu. My energy went into parenting and attending to survival, writing, and lecturing. I assumed different roles, but all the while my psyche was home in Hawaii. I needed to be two places at once, and writing was the bridge to link my worlds. Through my writing I could explain that, for me, Hawaii was not just a vacation playground, but an entry into a spirit world.

One night I had a dream that reflected the longing to be back in

Twilight

Hawaii and the nakedness I felt putting my first book into public hands. In the dream I visited a friend who was spending her days at work on an old typewriter in an attic, closed off from the world. I told my friend to leave that little world behind, but she said she was all right where she was.

Suddenly I was whisked out of the room and set down on the shore of a small cove. Behind me was a cliff bordering the beach. Turquoise foam rushed up to the sand and I ran down to the water's edge, where a giant sea turtle walked briskly by on two legs. As I followed him with my eyes, I saw an enormous clam on the sand with both shells wide open. 'My God!' I thought. 'It will be eaten. The clam must close up.' But the clam stayed open and I realized that we were safe in that haven. I heard my friend's voice from far away telling me that she could return there, whenever she wanted.

Upon waking I realized that part of me knew exactly what she was doing and chose to return to California to write a book and 'take care of business'. I wished, however, that I could fly back to paradise to stay.

My dream life continued to be as uncanny as it had been 3,000 miles away. I had a series of dreams that involved altered states and recurring images of UFOs. In one, I was in the process of moving to another apartment and was carrying a bookcase down the street when a man stopped me. He said that he had just taken the ceiling off of his head. I replied that I had done that before and suddenly experienced an openness, a huge expanse in my mind.

Later in the dream I met a group of people in Mill Valley. We were looking up at the stars and became dazzled by a spectacle of UFOs streaking across the sky over Mt Tamalpais. One man in our party began having trouble speaking. Although he sounded as if he were talking under water, he managed to tell us that his brain was affected by alien probes. I, too, began to feel strange – so dizzy.

When I awoke, I remembered the dream I had had on the Big Island in which I called down a Mother Ship with a trinket with James's face on it. After interacting with an alien in that dream, I had become dizzy. I wondered what the correlation was between the UFO image and the sensation of vertigo in both dreams.

In another of a series of dreams, I met secretly with a board of scientists, scholars and journalists in an underground hallway. We spoke quietly about our UFO connections, feeling the importance of our meeting and wondering if the information we each had would be seized and 'classified' by the government. After our meeting, we stepped out of the building on to a grassy plain surrounded by hills. A boy about ten years old ran along the hillside while a silver disk flew parallel to him, its shadow beside him. There was a strong magnetic pull to the aerial ship in my dream, which remained with me throughout the day after I awoke. Upon analyzing the dream, however, it didn't seem particularly significant, but splices of different movies I'd seen.

In September 1987 my friend Elizabeth and I met for tea at the Buttercup Café a few miles from the University of California, Berkeley campus. We talked about old times while enjoying almond croissants and mint tea. In the middle of our conversation I felt an inner radar go off and became distracted by a strangely familiar looking group of people seating themselves at the table next to us. They looked like typical university folk, scholarly and full of purpose. But I recognized the sober, bearded man sitting closest to me, and the intense young woman with long hair drawn tightly back seated next to him. Even more, I knew their energy the way an animal knows a scent.

I continued to keep one eye on them, until the man next to me gave me the 'sign'. He pulled a book out of his briefcase and propped it up on the table. So as not to be intrusive, I glanced over quickly. 'Pleiades'. That was all I saw, but I felt certain that these were the people in my dream about the meeting in an underground building.

I walked over to confront the mystery people at the next table. I told them I was involved with a UFO investigation of sorts and had noticed the book on the Pleiades. Were they involved with similar research? Each of the five looked at me keenly and said that they were. I took out my business card and passed it around, and they each pulled out one of their own. 'We must talk soon,' said one of the men. In the meantime Elizabeth had left our table and was paying the bill. She was visibly ruffled. Although we had been discussing uncanny experiences with spiritual teachers during our tea, she was again unnerved by the alien theme, especially when I told her about recognizing the UFO study group from a dream.

Even as I set the wheel in motion I wanted to know why I had dreamt about these people and then met them in the flesh. Perhaps I had been given the answer in the psychic channeling in Hawaii, in which I was told I would begin coming into contact with the star people with whom I was linked.

Peter, the man who had been seated next to me in the café, phoned the next evening. We talked for an hour, touching on experiences, but we were both evasive. When I told him about the dream from which I thought I recognized him, he didn't seem surprised, but invited me to meet his group, which, he said, had an academic approach to extraterrestrial phenomena. He also offered to bring me a video covering some of the notable UFO sightings in Europe. For some reason I wanted to back out. Things were moving too fast, just as they had when I recounted my dream to James. As in Hawaii, I wanted to be in control and know what the unseen forces were behind the dream and our meeting. I told Peter I had to bide my time and would call him when I wanted to delve further into our connection.

Months later I finally called Peter and we met for lunch at a local restaurant. I was hoping to experience a spiritual rapport with, and recognition from, a 'star person', someone with whom I had a special bond. But when we met, we were just two people with a mutual interest, sharing stories about the sightings we had had, finding interesting parallels. There was no soul spark. I had expected some profound link after seeing him in a dream, then recognizing him in the café. That I had dreams about UFOs was not surprising, but meeting the people from the dream surely was.

Perhaps the most interesting experience Peter told me about occurred when he described his spirit guide to a friend, and tiny lights flashed in the sky as if in response. This reminded me of a remarkably similar experience of my own, which had begun on Hallowe'en when I decided to listen to the tape recording of my psychic reading in Hilo. Although frequent dreams of UFOs followed me to the mainland, I had been denying the relevance of the symbolism in my pedestrian life. Living a more mundane reality in California, it seemed unbelievable to me that I had felt I was

Volcanic Visions

contacted by aliens in a vision and through psychic transmission. I turned on the tape recorder and lay back, trying to recall the feeling invoked in the mediumistic 'reading'.

Listening to 'Ashtar', I effortlessly relaxed and drifted into a state of autosuggestion, self-hypnosis induced by the voice patterns of the medium. When 'Cassiopeia's' voice came through, I was in a deeply altered state, and it seemed to me that there was a softening of energy around me and a shimmering in the air. Then I witnessed or imagined beautiful blue lights flitting around the room. Each light appeared as a flash of color moving quickly from one place to another. At one point an entire wall lit up in blue-violet. When the tape came to an end, the light was no longer present. All became visually quiet.

As I turned off the tape recorder, there was a loud knock on the door. It was Carrie, my next door neighbor. We had had a conversation the day before about our trips to Hawaii, and she had told me about the supernatural phenomena she had witnessed there, which she also attributed to the extraordinary environment of the islands. I had told her some of my own experiences, but shied away from saying anything about aliens.

Now, as Carrie sat down, she told me in her Southern drawl, 'After we talked, I started looking through my memos of Hawaii and pulled out this letter I wrote on the trip home and never sent.' She handed me a letter she had written to her boyfriend in which she summarized a film she had watched on the plane. I read the last line over and over, thinking I must not be reading it correctly: 'The girl looked up at the sky, and saw the constellation Cassiopeia. It was so beautiful!'

Carrie turned to me. 'Do you know anything about the mythology of Cassiopeia?'

I looked at her in amazement. 'If you only knew how coincidental it is that you should ask –' Before I could say more, a brilliant blue-violet light lit up a large area of the front wall.

'Wow!' Carrie cried out.

'You saw it?!'

'Yes! What was it?'

'It's unnerving,' I said.

We had a lot to talk about and I'm not quite sure what Carrie made of it all.

★

Twilight

Two months after listening to the tape of Cassiopeia and seeing the flashing blue-violet lights, I had a phone conversation with Petey Stevens, that began around 11 p.m. and ended at about 2 a.m. When I got off the phone, I wasn't sleepy, but my head felt heavy, a sensation that comes on before a vision. Although wide awake and full of energy, I laid my head on the pillow and slipped into astral flight. As I opened my dream eyes a little feminine being flew by, her body iridescent, a glowing crescent moon on her head. Then a multitude of sounds manifested, evolving into a multi-sensory dance of geometric shapes emerging from each note. After only a few moments, the vision lifted and I sat up in bed. Perhaps the etheric lady with the crescent moon was one of my spirit guides. Cassiopeia? Isis? I wondered.

My experiences with the fourth dimension and with other people were intersecting more and more. What had been an individual phenomenon became part of a larger picture. It seems that multi-dimensional beings have some consistent patterns in the way they contact humans. As well as through 'close encounters', they have a repertoire of methods they use to communicate and make their presence known, such as sparkling lights, dreams, channelings, visions and telepathic communication.

Many months went by without any further unusual occurrences. Then one night I was shaken from sleep at 3 a.m. by a loud bang against my bedroom window. My heart raced as I sat up in bed and saw a brilliant beam of light shining through my window. I was alarmed by the noise that punctured my sleep, but was moved by the beauty of the light.

My heart still knocking, I took a flashlight and forced myself to investigate the source of the noise. Out on the balcony all I could find were flowers, plants and a few fallen leaves; there were no rocks or hard objects that could have been thrown against the window.

I went back to bed a little disturbed by the unexplained noise, and light. Eventually I fell asleep again, but at 4:30 another bang hit my bedroom window, this time sounding like the blow of a fist. I bolted upright in time to see a dazzling diamond light flash in the window. I went out to the balcony again, but, as before, there was

Volcanic Visions

no trace of a hard projectile that could have hit the window. And there was no one there. It seemed that something was determined to break into my three-dimensional world, even if it meant breaking into my dreams.

17

RETROSPECT

I sing fire and water
wood earth at my feet
wilder than hair-spalling wind
than lips searing embers
than eyes burning wide
I'm gone
Scorpio camp round to roam
the song of them
who do know
forever flaunching —
oh gypsies
long horned call
oh gypsies
wood woman calling you

The events that took place in Hawaii, as well as in Marin after my return from the island, prompted me to look at the extraterrestrial connections throughout my life.

When I was a child my fantasies always involved invisible 'others' who I expected to come and take me home to the other side of reality. Even though I was close to my family, I felt there was something very important missing.

My dad provided my earliest link to conscious knowledge of, and interest in, ETs. When I was six, my brother, Frank, and I went to visit him in Beaumont, California, where we spent part of every summer. One evening, after a hot near-the-desert day, as we enjoyed the cooling temperature, drinking cream sodas and munching on ginger snaps, my dad told us about an experience he had had a couple of weeks before. He had been out for an evening stroll on one of the dark country roads. As he passed cows grazing in the

Volcanic Visions

darkness on the other side of the fence, the road he was walking down suddenly became lit brighter than day. Dad looked all around for the source, until he spotted silver disks in the sky. They appeared, then disappeared within the twinkling of an eye. The year was 1956, a hot era for UFOs.

My father became obsessed with reading science fiction and non-fiction that focused on ET contact stories, a reaction shared by many people who have had a 'contact' experience of any kind. Throughout the summer we watched sci-fi movies on TV together, and during one film Dad sat forward on the couch, pointing with intensity to bizarre images on the screen. Giving me a pat on the leg, he said, 'Look at that! Look at what they're doing,' while a strange-looking abductor placed a long needle in the back of the abductee's neck. Later scenes showed a deep scar left on the man's neck. I was somewhat traumatized by the movie and didn't understand my dad's enthusiasm. I was certain that those 'others' did not represent the kindred I was searching for.

When the movie was over, I fussed with my dad's collar, which was sticking up, and noticed a deep scar on the back of his neck. It had probably been there all my years, but seeing it at that moment, I got chills. When I asked my dad about it, he gave me an acceptable explanation: 'During the war a shell was lodged in my neck and left the scar.' When I went home to my mother, and asked her about the scar, she said she had never seen it.

In searching through my past for experiences connected to extra-terrestrials and to people who had awareness beyond the third dimension, I remembered other incidents.

At twenty-three, my boyfriend and I planned to create a lifestyle together in the wild. Our first idea was to join a community of people in the Santa Monica mountains who sustained themselves by running an organic farm. Rick and I and two other couples drove up to explore the possibilities. When we arrived, the farm was strangely quiet. No one came to greet us, as we thought was arranged; in fact, there was no one in sight. We walked around and looked for the lake and waterfall we had been told was on the property. When we came to where they should have been, we found a huge dry cement pit. I turned on a water spout nearby: out came a large spider, but not a drop of water.

Retrospect

We were becoming increasingly unnerved. Although the mountain was natural, the 'community' setting was not. But, as we had come for an outing at least, we didn't want to leave without a night under the stars. Towards evening we laid out sleeping bags between the trees and decided to take a walk before dark.

We walked for several minutes, hoping that we might still run into a resident, but were surprised when out of the seemingly deserted forest an elderly man approached us on a small tractor. 'You are all to report for work tomorrow morning,' he said tersely, his face rigid, and drove away. We stared at each other, shocked by this bizarre 'greeting' and by the discovery that someone had been aware of our presence all along, although the rest of the community remained hidden from us. Then we snapped to and discussed leaving as soon as possible – whatever was going on, it was not what we had come there for. But we decided to stay just long enough to watch the stars come out and view the night sky from the mountaintop.

We sat together talking in our little encampment among the trees. It grew dark quickly. Just as we got up to go into the clearing to view the night sky, we heard an ominous sound, an aggravating drone above the trees. We looked up and saw a long, dark cigar-shaped vehicle, just barely discernible in the dark, hovering above where we had been sitting. Staring at the strange object for a few moments, we were quick in our consensus, without verbalizing it. We grabbed our things, piled into the car and drove quickly down the mountain. As we descended, we began to talk again. The impression we all had was that there was a sinister presence in the vehicle in the sky.

The next year I went up to Mount Shasta in northern California, to stay with friends for several weeks. In contrast to that somewhat bizarre occasion in the Santa Monica Mountains, there my thought processes became more refined, and I perceived a luminous quality in the people I met and in the environment. Even though it is common to experience a heightened appreciation of beauty and a transcendental opening in such a power spot, this dormant volcano was the strongest magnetic vortex I had experienced until that time.

While sharing a 'sweat' in an outdoor sweat lodge, people who had lived on the mountain for many years told stories about meeting 'the Mu', a lost colony of wise ones who lived in the mountain. The folklore was similar to that I would later encounter on Hawaii. According to the local legend, many of the Mu had migrated from the continent before it went down, heeding the prophecies of its doom. As in Hawaiian legends, the Mount Shasta folklore credited the Mu with tremendous powers, including the ability to fly in space craft. Supposedly, their descendants were living 'in' the mountain now and were responsible for the high vibratory field in the region. Their mission was to accelerate the spiritual evolution of our planet. They were sighted from time to time, and were described as human in appearance, tall and regal, with magnetic eyes and long, flowing clothes. Sometimes lights were seen around the mountain, or disk-like ships that slipped out from clouds, and seemed to disappear over Shasta's dome.

Perhaps it is not coincidental that the Mount Shasta stories about the exodus and relocation of the Mu are similar to those recorded by the Hawaiians. Perhaps the spiritual teachers on Mu migrated to the mountaintops and volcanic peaks around the world, knowing them to be power spots and doorways through which the guardians travel in their airships. It is rumored that in Mauna Kea, Mount Shasta, Mount Fuji, the Himalayas and the Andes the Guardians have established schools where they transmit the original primordial teachings for the elevation of humankind.

As I reflected on many of my earlier life experiences and dreams, of which a few are mentioned here, it seemed to me that external events occur to support the internal process in the movement towards self-realization. The extraordinary experiences that have simultaneously punctured and punctuated my reality have created holes in my world, through which, if I choose, I enter other dimensions. Without following the lead of the inner world, encounters with the non-ordinary leave holes or gaps. They remain as mysteries that appear frightening, because a reality with which I'm not familiar lurks on the other side. However, after having a glimpse of realities that previously were invisible, my perceptions can never be seamless and third-dimensional again. Eye-openers in my childhood and in my earlier adult life, as well as the events in Hawaii, have led me to a new inner terrain.

18

THE MYTHIC ZONE

*The moon is full
the stars are hung
in perfect symmetry
lighting the way home*

In a circular hut of riotous colored flowers – fuchsia, magenta, tangerine, and gold – I inhaled the glorious sun and scents that streamed through translucent petal walls. My mind and skin were drenched in brilliant, sensual color of a Gauguin fantasy.

When I awoke I wanted to sink my roots in volcanic soil and to wrap the color of the Impressionistic dream around me. Since the 7.1 earthquake in 1989, I've become restless on California ground, and think about the ephemerality of life. I seek paradise and long to feed my soul in a rain forest or in a waterfall along the Hamakua coastline. As a clairsentient, I receive psychic input from my senses and open to the touch of rain, the salt of the sea, the heat of the sun.

Rousseau dreams and the thoughts of the islands swelling inside me again, I called James in Kea'au. His voice was filled with warmth and openness, inviting images of ferns and orchids from his garden, and soft rain. As pictographic scenes from the wet side of Hawaii distilled through my phone, James shared with me feelings and insights for the first time since our UFO sighting on Mauna Kea. I was startled by his openness after a refusal to talk about the event when we last spoke. But, after three years, James was able to speak enthusiastically of the sighting, claiming that his world view has been altered since then.

James told me that he has continued with his medical practice and maintains a rather low-key lifestyle. To this day he doesn't understand his erratic behavior that night nor how he was led to the

Volcanic Visions

mountaintop, where we became witnesses to the enormous wheel of spinning lights. But he does remember, he said, 'being in a deep altered state'. Surfacing from the shock of feeling spirited up the mountain, he later came to the realization that his consciousness underwent a perceptible change: 'Gravity changed from ego to something deeper, closer to essence. As the center of gravity began to change, words like 'importance' and 'significance' took on a new meaning that is lighter and more substantial at the same time. Things that used to bother me no longer carry the same weight.'

Recently, James told me, he had had another experience that intensified his awareness that something important exists outside of his ordinary point of reference. Driving back from South Point one day, he felt some 'presence' take him outside of himself, as if something within him had shifted. He doesn't remember exactly what happened to him, but he feels that he was altered in some essential way, as during the 'convergence' on Mauna Kea. In what sounded like a 'born again' testimonial, he told me that he now feels an active, tangible presence in his reality.

We had made contact together with some alien force and been touched again, separately, in different ways, by some hidden intelligence that seems to be altering our world view.

For me in the three years since I left Hawaii there were experiences in which those from the other side broke into my dreams and waking. But most of the time was spent on the mundane, even though something within me had subtly changed. I'd had evidence of the guardians weaving their way into my life, but I had the need again to prove their presence in my life. I wait as others wait for the 'Big One', an earthquake that will rearrange our state, and am aware of the daily escalation of international and national crises. On the island I came to believe that I was not alone in attempts to emerge from a looking-glass house. The 'butterfly people' were giving me messages from the other side. The ultraterrestrials who have left the cocoon of three-dimensional awareness behind are able to communicate from many levels and planes of existence.

In Hawaii I witnessed a circular luminous object appearing from the sky, shattering the illusion that it existed only in imagination. And in California I saw beautiful flashing lights when the name of

The Mythic Zone

my guide was mentioned. But in a shaky world I needed confirmation again that the guardians exist, and I petitioned, as others have petitioned their gods and guardian angels before me; 'Cassiopeia... Ashtar – if you exist, manifest in some way. Please give me a sign you are present in my world.'

I became restless, even peevish on that mild autumn night. For the first time since I had lived in the hills of Fairfax I took a walk at night down the dark road overlooking the quiet town below. As I strolled down the steep hill, I listened to baying dogs calling to each other and looked at the houses lit along the hillside at a distance ahead. I didn't go far, because I was slightly apprehensive walking in the dark alone and thought it was probably futile to petition the night for answers. I walked back up the hill again and stopped at a clearing where there were no trees nor houses to gaze down at the little town wedged between two rows of hills. As I looked over at the opposing hills, my eyes were attracted to a light that hung suspended behind the town.

A single golden light. I stood there motionless trying to determine its source. Not an airplane. A searchlight on a helicopter? I didn't think so – it was so perfectly still. I stood with rapt attention, breathing softly. 'You're here,' I thought. 'Please come closer.' Seemingly in response, the light expanded and became a brilliant, shining gold object in the sky. As I gazed at the luminous globe, the tension and frustration I had held in that evening lifted and a beautiful presence filled me with quiet joy. I stood looking out into the night, reaffirmed of that sacred presence. Slowly, the light grew smaller, until it was just a tiny beam and then was no more. But I knew the source was not far away.

The next day I called a small local airport and asked an air controller about what I had seen. 'Could have been a searchlight from a rescue 'copter that was sent to the headlands,' he said. 'Except for the color – 'copters don't use gold lights.'

Someday I may find another explanation for the gold light, but for now, it seems too synchronistic to be a coincidence. The pattern was familiar. On Hawaii, my friends and I felt called to a mountain-top and mentally called down a Mother Ship. A sparkling sphere of lights appeared as if in response to our petition, or perhaps we had responded to its siren call. Similarly, that night in Fairfax I felt a need to contact the guardians and called upon them to appear. With an inner prompting to walk down a dark road, I was led to witness a mysterious golden light in the sky. Both encounters with unidentified light sources brought about a perceptible mood change and I felt a rarefied presence enter my awareness as if a transmission from the numinous.

When I returned home from my walk, I slipped back in the house feeling peaceful and light. Josh, who had been absorbed in a TV show when I left, had apparently not heard me when I said I was going out for a walk. 'Where have you been?!' he demanded.

'Out for a walk,' I said, smiling.

'That's weird,' he said, shaking his head. 'You never take walks alone at night.'

I've spoken to several people about my sighting on Mauna Kea, several of whom told me that they too had contact with a UFO the night of the Convergence. One young woman had been at Haleakala, on Maui, that night for the celebration, along with hundreds of other people. She had felt an inner prompting leading her away from the throngs to a spot where she remembers seeing several spinning lights in formation. A man told me he had been living on Kauai and felt an urgent need to visit Molokai on August 16. He followed his intuition until he arrived at a spot where he saw shining disks flitting across the sky. Another man I spoke to was led away from a designated power spot in the state of Washington and came to a place where he also witnessed flying disks the night of the Convergence.

What we all have in common is that we were led away from a larger group the night of August 16, 1987 and had sightings of spinning wheels, disks or spheres of lights. On some level an initiation took place, which we may not all fully comprehend yet, but seeds were planted that will lead us to the next step in our journey.

During the alignment of Venus, Mars, Mercury and Regulus many other people gathered to recharge the planet with light, and to infuse the cosmos and Earth with their love. Perhaps many who participated have become initiated as light-bearers and will be illuminated pathfinders in the fifth world.

The Mythic Zone

The guardians continue to make contact on a personal level through the dream realm. Upon falling deeply asleep one night I travelled to Maui, where I was moved by the watercolor feel of dolphins and whales swimming along its mandala borders. The island was surrounded by cerulean sky, jade trees and brilliant bursts of fuchsia, hibiscus, creamy plumerias and pikake gold. As I drank in the softness, a longing began for a glimpse of the land where magma pours out of the seams of the Earth, ignited with incandescent light. I felt called back to the black and crimson of Hawaii – the pulsating, burning mountain of Kilauea.

I looked out to sea, longing to return to a Persephone myth deep in the Earth, walking along Pele's razor edge. Suddenly, a bright green sea turtle rose up out of the ocean, towering high above me. A woman appeared next to me and said, 'Beware of the stinger!' I looked at where she was pointing and saw a whirling blade of energy at the turtle's front base. The creature brushed my leg with the spinning projectile, sending an electrical charge up my leg. I felt no pain and no fear.

When I woke up I felt that I had been visited by a sentient presence, but assumed it was born from my unconscious. I thought about who the archetype was and its message to me. The carapace was a mandala shape, symbol of wholeness and integration. Reminding me of the 'saucer' shape, both were images of alien entities emerging from the unknown, from the mysterious depths of sea and space. The stinger was the vehicle for transmitting and inseminating energy, analogous to a yogi releasing energy during an initiation of a student, the brilliantly lit space ship on Mauna Kea, as well as the golden light in the Fairfax hills, transmitting energy to me. The whirling motion of the stinger seemed reminiscent, too, of the whirling wheel of lights on Mauna Kea.

Numerous world cultures have different interpretations of the mysteries of the turtle. Native American traditions view the turtle as a symbol of Mother Earth. An Indian group in the Caribbean have legends about a mysterious turtle mother who guides her clan to safe harbor when greedy fishermen take too many, threatening the extinction of the species. The Hindu religion records that the second incarnation of Vishnu, god of preservation, was a giant turtle who held up the Earth. The ancient Chinese claimed that the

Volcanic Visions

turtle had the highest human virtues written on its back, and included 'turtle' as one of their earliest written words.* According to some myths, the turtle's back is the vault of the sky, the spiritual realm representing the yang, or male energy, in the universe. The turtle's carapace, they say, is marked with constellations. The belly of the turtle represents the yin, the female principle, in the universe, all that is created or manifest. As the turtle carries a mythic map on its back, it is for each culture and person who meets the archetype to decode its message.

Perhaps an alien, a shape shifter from another world, the dream messenger appears in diverse forms as a catalyst transmitting electromagnetic energy to awaken in the dreamer awareness of a multi-dimensional reality. Although its natural home is the sea, as a shamanic figure the dream turtle is a reptile and land dweller as well. Perhaps the turtle's challenge to me was to learn a flexibility and versatility in traveling to different planes of consciousness, living in the outer world while exploring the inner terrains. The dream turtle might be the Turtle Mother, an initiating guardian who infused me with her energy to gain wholeness in the interior and exterior worlds as she has, with a mandala, a medicine shield on her back.

On one of the oldest silver coins found in Greece, dating from about the fifth century BC, there is an image of the sea turtle engraved on one side, with Aphrodite on the other. Aphrodite had an affinity with the sea turtle because she too was of the ocean, born from the sea's foam. Also known as Venus, mother of Eros, goddess of love and the arts, Aphrodite drew her inspiration from the oceanic world, from the unconscious depths. As she filled her mind with dreams from the sea and of the land, Atlantis, a jewel in the sea, she rode across the ocean, on the turtle's strong, broad back.

Ruled by Venus, under the sign of Taurus, in the twelfth house of Pisces, I too have an affinity with the sea turtle. The turtle of my dreams knows well the earthly realm, as it comes to shore to mate, the female spawning her eggs on the wet sandy beach. And, as a

*Martha Reeves, *The Total Turtle*, New York, Thomas Cromwell Co., 1975, p. 66.

The Mythic Zone

messenger of the spirit world, from the Neptunian depths the sea turtle brings mystical dreams.

Traveling interdimensionally in their circular ships, the winged ones continue to tap into my dreams and appear in different forms in my waking. Whether external realities or deep aspects of the mind, they hover near the mythic doorway leading to the upper worlds.

While exploring a personal mythology, traveling the byways of an inner and outer terrain, initiations illuminate the spiral staircase that leads to the mystic zone beyond finite perception or understanding. The Hawaiians call that place Po. Whether directions are read on a sea turtle's back, on a star map or in a prophet's cryptic script, exploration can take one to a volcanic island or down a country road. We are individually and collectively finding the way to enlightenment, we are finding the way home.

On a path in the foothills of a mountain the air was clear and scented with growing herbs among the trees. I looked out at the lapis bowl of sky, starlit and full of meditative silence. Then, suddenly, from out of the surrounding space a flying object broke through the darkness and swooped over my head. The vehicle was *en route* to a retreat below the mountain, I thought in the dream.

I continued on the path and was met by a donkey cart coming up the road from the retreat. Inside were a group of people whom I could see clearly enough to feel excitement as I looked at their luminous faces and crystal eyes. I knew who they were, and the woman seated near the edge of the wagon leaned over and smiled as though she knew me. 'Will you join us?' she asked. I embraced them with my heart and said, 'Soon.' I listened to the sound of the tinkling donkey bells as the cart traveled up the road.

19

RING OF FIRE

Volcano

Planted deep in the womb
grown from molten red chambers
an eruption in a lava heave
is running down my mountain

Flashing eyes
lightening touch
thundering thighs
burning red lips
transform a hot primal night

From the beginning of my quest, the volcano was the primal power, the siren call that beckoned, requesting I leave all but my son and my soul to follow the smoke of Kilauea. Even now in the hills of Marin County, watching the red hawk soar past my window, I return to the primordial world of molten black fields and incandescent streams of lava in the night. Like a moth attracted to a flame, I imagine flying over a fiery fissure, a phoenix ascended from ashes.

On the Big Island I was psychically hooked up to Kilauea. Opening myself to the consciousness of Pele, I felt the flow of *pahoehoe* lava along my spine, and the stir of ancestral memory bubbling in my mind. I expected initiation to be sudden and complete, like an overnight eruption and building of a mountain. But I found that stages of spiritual initiation usually occur over a period of time with a series of events, like the gradual growth of a volcano from repeated lava flows. Forces of change may brew unseen for long periods until the right alchemical combination of energies and awareness is achieved. Then, as if by magic, the volcano grows in someone's cornfield; an individual transits from ordinary to extraordinary awareness and relationships to life.

Ring of Fire

As the volcano smolders within me, brewing revolutionary and transformative change I feel akin to people living on burning mountains, witnessing daily the crumbling and resurrection of their world. On the Big Island and in volcanic regions around the globe the triune mysteries of birth, death and rebirth are intertwined with artistic expression, philosophic perspective and cultural rites of passage. In Indonesia, one of the most volatile regions along the Ring of Fire, the residents experience the presence of their gods in every dimension of their lives. When the gods are sleeping, and only smoke is seen issuing from the mouths of the giants – Krakatoa, Agung and other members of the volcanic dynasty – the people of the islands bring to life the drama of the gods in animistic dance and shadow puppetry. Behind a fire-lit screen ornamented puppets on sticks incite the imagination of the audience, dramatizing the twin mysteries of inner and outer reality. While villagers play, the fire gods sleep, until the awesome moment when they rouse themselves with a roar, blasting apart the stage and flickering screen.

Devotees of fire gods everywhere know the fragility of living on the razor's edge – the ripest, most luxuriant, most dangerous place to be. Day and night they experience the mystic rites of their god, who is creator and destroyer of their world. The prophesy has finally come to pass: Pele has taken Kalapana. The people there know, as do the people of Java and Japan, that they must be prepared at any moment to offer their homes and their lives to their deity.

As a catalyst, the volcano is an archetype of upheaval, revolution and transformation. Given the face of a goddess, it is a living entity responsible for the growth of our planet from inception. As a metaphor, the volcano resides in the human body as Mother Kundalini, an eruptive power that shoots up the spine, bringing about metamorphosis in body and mind.

Both the flying disk and a volcano's caldera are circles of power, mandalas of transformation. The living entities spiriting them are ultraterrestrials, beyond the limits of human understanding, embodying and manifesting the extraordinary. Teachers of the terrestrial and extraterrestrial worlds, they trigger psychological and spiritual transformation in their initiates. Terra, our womb mother, is the root teacher, the first mandala we must circumambulate to learn the mysteries of the other worlds. The guardians of the earth and

Volcanic Visions

the other dimensions open us up like ripened flowers as we realize our wisdom potential. In concert with the cosmic whisperings quickening our spirit, the Earth experience is the mulch, the raw material from which we obtain initiation, transmuting our dross into gold.

In the bubbling of the magma and the pounding of the sea the elemental teachers speak through the body, touch the mind through the psychic channels as through erogenous zones. The *aumakuas*, or guardians, of the earth, the air, water and fire each have their lessons that further the evolution of the human form and mind. For each elemental form there is a corresponding psychological disposition and awareness. The aspects of the mind are personified by the volcanoes, lightning, thunder, the sea and earth. The teachings of the elements are played out most dramatically by Pele, the goddess of the triple mysteries of creation, destruction and rebirth.

It is through initial conflict and opposition that creation and transformation take place. From out of the early chaos brought about by interaction with disparate elements new life forms are created. From tremendous pressure and conflict the Earth is born; from exploding gases, fire and air, a seething, quivering sea of magma is created. Volcanic waste becomes seed for fertile soil, nurturing exotic flowers and luscious fruits. From out of the explosions and chaos of an erupting volcano, paradise eventually is born.

The violent yet ecstatic pangs of volcanic birth have been likened to the spiritual birth that takes place when one is in the throes of labour, brought on by the *shakti* energy of the *kundalini* fire. As a macrocosmic *shakti*, Pele is an initiator igniting the *kundalini* in her initiates. She stirs up polarities in the personality, requiring her students to find reconciliation and balance. Enlightenment becomes attainable when the initiate returns from the depths and travels back up the spiral staircase with an integrated mind.

The stories of Pele and her tempestuous encounters with lovers, friends and foes are filled with overwhelming passion, jealousy, treachery and revenge. The tales dramatize the dramatic shadow side of the human personality, the anthropomorphic displays of a volcanic spirit. The shadow side provides power and a tremendous source of energy within the mind of one who successfully transmutes the fire born from internal chaos, negativity and contradiction.

Ring of Fire

Played out metaphorically in myths personifying the volcanic personality, the psychological and esoteric elements of these stories have inspired many.

In the mandala of the Ring of Fire the world is dominated by violent opposing forces and is shaken by a serpent power racing along grinding tectonic plates, surging through those who live within the seismic borders. As volcanoes blow, the world rocks and rolls, and social orders tumble and fall; it is a time of transformation, a change of our individual and collective mythologies. In the transition we are moving quickly along the razor's edge into the fifth world. Even as old world views collapse, new dimensions of consciousness are breaking through the rigid constructs and paradigms of the past. Throughout the transition there will be enough voltage to awaken many living at its reptilian center.

The alchemist masters and guardians are reminders that throughout the conflict and chaos of transition, we have the ability to use the erupting energy as alchemical mulch from which to transmute awareness ... even as a salamander descending into a burning cauldron, emerging with its tail in its mouth, tasting immortality. In our individual experience, as we consciously plunge deep into the primordial fire within, a porthole opens to the universe.

In a frightening dream, resolved through active imagination, a volcano stood towering directly behind me and a group of people scattered near the base looked at it as though it were the Eiffel Tower. 'It is alive,' I warned. 'At any moment it's going to erupt.' The ground began to shake and I realized that regardless how fast I ran, I couldn't move quickly enough to escape the eruption that was ready to break loose. So I stood, shaking, watching as fire and boulders began to fly. My fear and the power of the volcano kept me in place.

As the sky filled with magma, shards and rocks shooting like bullets, I waited for my end, but suddenly the magma, hot and viscous, poured through my crown like thick blood. I panicked – I wanted to scream and cry for help, but realized no one could help me. There was no way out. The lava continued its way down, caressing the inside of my head, gushing through my spine like a rich emollient. Then, at lightning speed, magma rushed upward, hemorrhaging from my head like a crimson geyser. Gasping and choking at the rapid movement into my

Volcanic Visions

brain, I cried out, witnessing the volcano, the earth, the sky torched by a translucent light – and the inside of my head ignited as a vivid terrain, a luminous foretaste of Po.

Epilogue

I went to the volcanic island on a vision quest in search of my own totem and spirit ally. I felt the presence of the indigenous spirits. The smoke of Pele is all-pervasive in that place on voggy days and nights. In vision before sleep I saw her fly over a smoldering cauldron, an incandescent fire pouring over the volcanic sides. I came to know, as when I was a child, an animistic reality populated by elementals, devas — a spirit in every natural form.

What was unexpected was that a non-animate archetypal image would make an appearance in my dreams, in vision and in waking. As a sphere with rotating electromagnetic lights, known only as a UFO, it penetrated my reality. The significance could have been as little as that of a cola bottle dropped from an airplane, made into a totem and cult of great spiritual import because it came from a mysterious source. In the 1980 Jamie Uys film *The Gods Must Be Crazy* the bushman who found the bottle as yet knew nothing of airplanes and the Pepsi generation.

I accept the idea that on some level we all create our own realities. Our interpretations of outer events reflect an inner belief system and are filtered through a subjective interpretation of appearances. To a large degree we draw to ourselves persons and events in accordance with our inner programing and predispositions, some of which are socially scripted, while other tendencies and proclivities are preconscious, or innate.

In my attempt to understand the UFO mythology that seemed to be emanating from my psychic infrastructure, as well as from a source outside of myself, I drew from disciplines that were relevant to the time and place, and offered cross-cultural perspectives of reality and of the extraterrestrial paradigm. Hawaiian mythology, Hopi and Mayan prophecies as they related to the Harmonic Convergence, Jungian transpersonal psychology and a contemporary UFO belief system conveyed by the channel gave varying interpretations of extraterrestrials and the archetype we know as a UFO. All

Volcanic Visions

of these points of view helped to create a background that influenced my perception and assessment of the wheel of lights.

In writing the story I found myself in a quandary as to which position to take as both the observer and the subject of my own experience. At times I wanted to approach paranormal manifestations the way an anthropologist in the field approaches a person on a medicine path, without preconditioned assessment of trance states and mystical experiences, and without ethnocentric superimposition. I wanted to take the dispassionate role, making observations, collecting data, reviewing internal and external encounters and events without personalization – reserving judgment because of lack of conclusive information, as in identifying the aerial object we viewed. But to take the role of observer created a dualistic position while engaging in a vision quest.

There was no easy reconciliation of the two hemispheres of the brain. During visionary episodes the right brain opened its psychic gates to direct intuitive experiences. The rhapsody and symbolic content created a synergistic breakthrough in consciousness. Each vision was a holistic reality, an attunement to another dimension, beyond need for explanation.

When I was no longer in an altered state, however, the rationalistic left brain came to the fore, requiring a context for the symbolism and a rational explanation for the feelings evoked while in trance. I tried to compartmentalize the material that emerged from the unconscious. But mythic material does not always fit into any previously known construct, even though I tried to relegate the vision of Pele and the UFO to the exclusive domain of the interior realms.

However, when the repetition of vision, dream and channeled UFO images were a prelude to external verifiable events, the subtext became magnified. The experiences followed an uncannily ordered pattern throughout my quest. As a preview, I had the vision of a UFO illuminated against the backdrop of a black volcanic mountain, followed by a dream of Dr James West, who appeared as an alien icon, the key to magnetizing a UFO.

The plot thickened with a channeled reading in which I was told I was continuing a telepathic communication with multidimensional beings that was established from other lifetimes. The medium

Epilogue

indicated that I would soon see a Mother Ship as verification that they were present in my world. Intellectually, the material was easily rejected at face value, but was unsettling when the prediction came to pass. It is difficult to know how to assess those messages that whisper from behind the veil, because perhaps at times the transmission is literal and at others is a chimera of the mind.

Dream images of a space ship turned into a startling bump on the head with reality when I walked into Ryan's eerily lit UFO room. When he showed me an elaborate sound system of his creation in the shape of a UFO, it was as if a message was being flashed with the repetition of the archetypal image. I didn't know how to decode or process the appearance of the symbol in relation to myself. Either I could easily overpersonalize the prophetic visions and dreams, as I at times was inclined to do, or assume a kind of disassociation from the validity of my own perceptions and those of people around me who also seemed influenced by the same elusive symbol.

Four times foretold, including by James the night before the Convergence, the physical appearance of the UFO came to pass. Like an image preserved on a reel of film, the mythic content was projected in climactic presentation on the top of a 13,000-foot volcano. In awe I viewed two amber headbeams floating above a silent titanic wheel of brilliant lights.

The left brain did not know what the right brain was doing, as if there was some trickery or illusion. In part, I went into denial of what I was seeing, but the sighting was no apparition, as attested by four others. The three adults were well accustomed to the use of their critical faculties. The one variable was that James was affected by a hypnotic altered state the night before the sighting. As if a precursor to the actual sighting, he seemed 'programmed' to get us to the mountain on time. Out of the five, to my knowledge, it was only James and I who were preconditioned for the experience and who felt a profound import and recognition when seeing manifest the actual ship.

In part I rejected the gift of vision, the totem from other worlds, by leaving the island abruptly, overwhelmed by the mix of myth and reality. I left before I could process the experience in the environmental context in which I had encountered it. On some level I said to the unseen forces, 'Give me something that I can cherish and

Volcanic Visions

understand.' But the mythic world springs from the unconscious and from hidden dimensions, and the archetypal content does not necessarily disappear from dreams – or from reminders in the waking state – once it has emerged. There must be time, regardless of how long it takes, for a psychosynthesis of the symbology and an understanding of the spirits that one meets.

When I went to a volcanic terrain and asked the spirits to give me a vision, I received two: the form of an illuminated goddess flying over a burning mountain, and a spirited flying object on top of Mauna Kea; two luminaries appearing at different times in the same psychic sky.

Dreams, numerology, the tarot and astrology are mythic maps reflecting the psychic dominants in a person's life. Contemplating the meaning of my visions on Hawaii, I recently turned to the astrological mandala – the spinning wheel reflecting archetypes and their karmic position in one's life. The two most prominent configurations in my chart are the moon midheaven, the chart's highest point, and the planet Pluto nadir, the lowest point in the wheel. As with lucid dreams, the symbolic content within these two astrological images creates layer upon layer of meaning. Mauna Kea volcano, the site where I witnessed a UFO, is the highest seamount in the world, metaphorically at midheaven. Kilauea volcano, from which a vision of the goddess Pele was inspired, gives scientists a view down into the interior workings of the Earth, at the metaphoric nadir.

Two initiating guardians, the moon and Pluto, are like sentinels juxtaposed in my chart. How like a UFO is the luminous circular moon. With a moon midheaven, perhaps it is not surprising to dream of a tree that gives birth to luminous moon eggs. The moon is the doorway to the womb, point of entry to the soul. The birth goddess is the luminary who rules the unconscious, disseminating visions, prophecies and creativity.

At the other end of the spectrum, the goddess Pele, at my astrological nadir, is the doorway to the tomb and resurrection. The counterpart to Pluto, she is the guardian of death and rebirth; her domain, the underworld, from which volcanoes spring. She creates tremendous depth of perception.

My moon is on the cusp of Aquarius, the astrological age into

Epilogue

which we are moving. Aquarius, ruled by the planet Uranus, brings with it a change of symbology. 'They are, it seems, changes in the constellation of psychic dominants, of the archetypes, or "gods" as they used to be called, which bring about, or accompany, long-lasting transformations of the collective psyche.'* As we approach Aquarius, sign of electromagnetic currents, interdimensional awareness, egalitarianism and parapsychology, new visions and archetypal forms are manifesting. The UFO is perhaps one of the first cosmic insignias to appear, as a prelude to the new astrological age, representing other worlds and a consciousness to explore that is beyond the range of our previous experience.

The volcano is one of the other archetypal dominants in our present age. Witnessed by more than a few, Pele rises up out of the Earth's cauldron, lighting the sky with her volcanic visions. Symbol for upheaval, freedom and transformation, the energies are expressed through eruptions, earthquakes and changes in the Earth's physical and social atmosphere. As one face of Gaia, the volcano goddess is the wrathful, cleansing deva who makes rectifications for the damage caused by those who rape and pollute the Earth, desecrating her sanctuary. Seen anthropomorphically, she is the warrior goddess who fights oppression on every level and ignites the desire for autonomy and the dignity of life in all its forms. As an archetypal dominant, the volcanic spirit is spreading to every sector of society in the call for human and animal rights, and is moving as a magma tide through the human heart. The upheaval and disintegration of cultural, political and spiritual orders is part of the Earth's atonement, making way for a return to the sacred, and the healing, regenerative rays of the goddess.

On a vision quest the medium opens the gateway to receiving the radio waves of archetypal dominants in the psychic heavens. After initially scanning through the cosmic soup for a broadcast, the seeker locks into a strong signal and tunes out for a time the static that ordinarily interferes with reception. The archetypes whose energies I registered during my quest are dynamically part of a

---

*C. G. Jung, *Flying Saucers: A Modern Myth of Things Seen in the Sky*, New York, Harcourt, Brace & Co., 1959, p. xii.

Volcanic Visions

personal and collective mythology. They have become like portals opening me up to other dimensions. Both the volcano and the UFO are mandala mirrors reflecting the mysteries of creation and the cosmos.

Appendix

Mythmakers place the legend of Mu somewhere in a vast period between 100,000 BC and 12,000 BC, when a civilization with a metaphysically powered technology existed on a large continent in the Pacific. Sources differ wildly on the time span. From books such as *The Kumulipo*, *Tales of the Night Rainbow* and *Children of the Rainbow*, derived from oral histories and ancient texts, a story is pieced together in which extraterrestrial denizens brought into being a human progeny who populated the now-lost continent of Mu, which was destroyed during cataclysmic volcanic eruptions and flooding.

This myth conflicts with geological studies from which scientists postulate that the Hawaiian islands developed individually into discrete land masses during successive volcanic eruptions: 'The Pacific Plate is not stationary; it has been sliding slowly northwestward, and as each island was formed it was carried away from the "hot spot", and another formed in its place. It is this hot spot that the still developing underwater seamount Loihi, and the Big Island now share.'*

The empirical foundation upon which modern science is built seems at times irrefutable. However, new discoveries can drastically alter interpretations of what previously seemed hard evidence for a particular theory. As there has been found much truth in even the most fanciful myth, as in the legend of Troy, it is not unthinkable that a large land mass buried beneath the Pacific will some day be discovered, with evidence that at least some of the Hawaiian islands were once a part of the greater whole.

The difference between myth and fact becomes blurred when we speak of vanished or hidden civilizations such as Mu and Atlantis, or

---

*Herb K. Kane, *Pele, Goddess of Hawaii's Volcanoes*, Captain Cook, Hawaii, The Kawainui Press, 1987, p. 56.

Volcanic Visions

invisible islands populated by the gods. But it is the vision of heavenly worlds and of a transcendent reality that propels us further into the mysteries of the universe.

Select Bibliography

Anderson, Johannes E., *Myths and Legends of the Polynesians*, Tokyo, Charles E. Tuttle Co., 1969

Beckwith, Martha W., *Hawaiian Mythology*, Honolulu, University of Hawaii Press, 1970

Beckwith, Martha W. (ed.), *The Kumulipo: A Hawaiian Creation Chant*, Chicago, University of Chicago Press, 1951

Berenholtz, Jim, *International Sacred Sites Festival Notes*, Maui, Hawaii, 1987

Childress, David Hatcher, *Lost Cities of Ancient Lemuria and the Pacific*, Stelle, Ill., Adventures Unlimited Press, 1987

Ching, Linda and Shurley, Bruce, *Hawaiian Goddesses*, Honolulu, Hawaiian Goddesses Publishing Co., 1987

Churchward, James, *The Lost Continent of Mu*, Albuquerque, NM, BE Books, 1987

Evans-Wentz, W. Y. (ed.), *Tibetan Book of the Dead*, London, Oxford University Press, 1960

Evans-Wentz, W. Y., *Tibetan Book of the Great Liberation*, Oxford, Oxford University Press, 1968

Frazer, James G., *Myths of the Origins of Fire*, New York, Hacher Arts Books, 1930

Gimbutas, Marija, *The Goddesses and Gods of Old Europe*, Berkeley, University of California Press, 1982

Grof, Stanislav, and Grof, Christina, *Spiritual Emergency: When Personal Transformation Becomes a Crisis*, Los Angeles, Jeremy Tarcher Inc., 1989

Jamal, Michele, 'The Sacred Fire', *Psi Research Journal*, San Francisco, 1985

Jamal, Michele, *Shape Shifters: Shaman Women in Contemporary Society*, London, Routledge & Kegan Paul, 1987; reprinted by Penguin Arkana, 1988

Jung, C. G., *Collected Works*, Vol. 9, Pt I, *Archetypes and the Collective Unconscious*, 2nd edn., Princeton, NJ, Princeton University Press, 1969

Jung, C. G., *Flying Saucers: A Modern Myth of Things Seen in the Sky*, New York, Harcourt, Brace & Co., 1959

Kane, Herb K., *Pele, Goddess of Hawaii's Volcanoes*, Captain Cook, Hawaii, The Kawainui Press, 1987

Lee, Pali, and Willis, Koko, *Tales of the Night Rainbow*, Honolulu, Night Rainbow Publishing Co., 1987

Long, Max Freedom, *The Huna Code in Religions*, Marina del Rey, CA., De Vorss & Co., 1987

MacDonald, George, *Volcanoes in the National Parks in Hawaii*, Honolulu, Tongg Publishing Co., 1982

Mann, E. Edward, *Orgone, Reich, and Eros*, New York, Simon & Schuster, 1973

Melville, Leinani, *Children of the Rainbow: The Religions, Legends and Gods of Pre-Christian Hawaii*, Wheaton, Ill., Theosophical Publishing House, 1969

Morrison, Boone, *Images of the Hula*, Volcano, Hawaii, Summit Press, 1983

Mullins, Joe, *The Goddess Pele*, Honolulu, Tongg Publishing Co., 1977

Neumann, Erich, *The Great Mother: An Analysis of the Archetype*, Princeton, NJ, Princeton University Press, 1974

Reeves, Martha, *The Total Turtle*, New York, Thomas Crowell Co., 1975

Rudloe, Jack, *Time of the Turtle*, New York, Alfred Knopf, 1979

Sjoo, Monica, *The Ancient Religion of the Greatest Cosmic Mother of All*, Trondheim, Norway, Rainbow Press, 1981

Spretnak, Charlene, *Lost Goddesses of Early Greece: A Collection of Pre-Hellenic Mythology*, Boston, Beacon Press, 1981

Targ, Russell and Harary, Keith, *The Mind Race: Understanding and Using Psychic Abilities*, New York, Villard Books, 1984

Walton, Bruce, *Mount Shasta, Home of the Ancients*, Mokelumne Hill, CA, Health Research, 1985

Waters, Frank, *Book of the Hopi*, New York, Ballantine Books, 1963

Westervelt, William, *Hawaiian Legends of Volcanoes*, Tokyo, Charles E. Tuttle Co., 1963

Wilhelm, Richard and Jung, C. G., *Secret of the Golden Flower: A Chinese Book of Life*, New York, Harcourt Brace Jovanovich Inc., 1962

ARKANA – NEW-AGE BOOKS FOR MIND, BODY AND SPIRIT

A selection of titles

With over 200 titles currently in print, Arkana is the leading name in quality new-age books for mind, body and spirit. Arkana encompasses the spirituality of both East and West, ancient and new, in fiction and non-fiction. A vast range of interests is covered, including Psychology and Transformation, Health, Science and Mysticism, Women's Spirituality and Astrology.

If you would like a catalogue of Arkana books, please write to:

Arkana Marketing Department
Penguin Books Ltd
27 Wright's Lane
London W8 5TZ

ARKANA – NEW-AGE BOOKS FOR MIND, BODY AND SPIRIT

A selection of titles

Neal's Yard Natural Remedies Susan Curtis, Romy Fraser and Irene Kohler

Natural remedies for common ailments from the pioneering Neal's Yard Apothecary Shop. An invaluable resource for everyone wishing to take responsibility for their own health, enabling you to make your own choice from homeopathy, aromatherapy and herbalism.

Zen in the Art of Archery Eugen Herrigel

Few in the West have strived as hard as Eugen Herrigel to learn Zen from a Master. His classic text gives an unsparing account of his initiation into the 'Great Doctrine' of archery. Baffled by its teachings he gradually began to glimpse the depth of wisdom behind the paradoxes.

The Absent Father: Crisis and Creativity Alix Pirani

Freud used Oedipus to explain human nature; but Alix Pirani believes that the myth of Danae and Perseus has most to teach an age which offers 'new responsibilities for women and challenging questions for men' – a myth which can help us face the darker side of our personalities and break the patterns inherited from our parents.

Woman Awake: A Celebration of Women's Wisdom Christina Feldman

In this inspiring book, Christina Feldman suggests that it *is* possible to break out of those negative patterns instilled into us by our social conditioning as women: conformity, passivity and surrender of self. Through a growing awareness of the dignity of all life and its connection with us, we can regain our sense of power and worth.

Water and Sexuality Michel Odent

Taking as his starting point his world-famous work on underwater childbirth at Pithiviers, Michel Odent considers the meaning and importance of water as a symbol: in the past – expressed through myths and legends – and today, from an advertisers' tool to a metaphor for aspects of the psyche.

ARKANA – NEW-AGE BOOKS FOR MIND, BODY AND SPIRIT

A selection of titles

Weavers of Wisdom: Women Mystics of the Twentieth Century Anne Bancroft

Throughout history women have sought answers to eternal questions about existence and beyond – yet most gurus, philosophers and religious leaders have been men. Through exploring the teachings of fifteen women mystics – each with her own approach to what she calls 'the truth that goes beyond the ordinary' – Anne Bancroft gives a rare, cohesive and fascinating insight into the diversity of female approaches to mysticism.

Dynamics of the Unconscious: Seminars in Psychological Astrology Volume II Liz Greene and Howard Sasportas

The authors of *The Development of the Personality* team up again to show how the dynamics of depth psychology interact with your birth chart. They shed new light on the psychology and astrology of aggression and depression – the darker elements of the adult personality that we must confront if we are to grow to find the wisdom within.

The Myth of Eternal Return: Cosmos and History Mircea Eliade

'A luminous, profound, and extremely stimulating work . . . Eliade's thesis is that ancient man envisaged events not as constituting a linear, progressive history, but simply as so many creative repetitions of primordial archetypes . . . This is an essay which everyone interested in the history of religion and in the mentality of ancient man will have to read. It is difficult to speak too highly of it' – Theodore H. Gaster in *Review of Religion*

The Second Krishnamurti Reader Edited by Mary Lutyens

In this reader bringing together two of Krishnamurti's most popular works, *The Only Revolution* and *The Urgency of Change*, the spiritual teacher who rebelled against religion points to a new order arising when we have ceased to be envious and vicious. Krishnamurti says, simply: 'When you are not, love is.' 'Seeing,' he declares, 'is the greatest of all skills.' In these pages, gently, he helps us to open our hearts and eyes.

ARKANA – NEW-AGE BOOKS FOR MIND, BODY AND SPIRIT

A selection of titles

A Course in Miracles: The Course, Workbook for Students and Manual for Teachers

Hailed as 'one of the most remarkable systems of spiritual truth available today', *A Course in Miracles* is a self-study course designed to shift our perceptions, heal our minds and change our behaviour, teaching us to experience miracles – 'natural expressions of love' – rather than problems generated by fear in our lives.

Sorcerers Jacob Needleman

'An extraordinarily absorbing tale' – John Cleese.

'A fascinating story that merges the pains of growing up with the intrigue of magic ... constantly engrossing' – *San Francisco Chronicle*

Arthur and the Sovereignty of Britain: Goddess and Tradition in the Mabinogion Caitlín Matthews

Rich in legend and the primitive magic of the Celtic Otherworld, the stories of the *Mabinogion* heralded the first flowering of European literature and became the source of Arthurian legend. Caitlín Matthews illuminates these stories, shedding light on Sovereignty, the Goddess of the Land and the spiritual principle of the Feminine.

Shamanism: Archaic Techniques of Ecstasy Mircea Eliade

Throughout Siberia and Central Asia, religious life traditionally centres around the figure of the shaman: magician and medicine man, healer and miracle-doer, priest and poet.

'Has become the standard work on the subject and justifies its claim to be the first book to study the phenomenon over a wide field and in a properly religious context' – *The Times Literary Supplement*

ARKANA – NEW-AGE BOOKS FOR MIND, BODY AND SPIRIT

A selection of titles

Head Off Stress: Beyond the Bottom Line D. E. Harding

Learning to head off stress takes no time at all and is impossible to forget – all it requires is that we dare take a fresh look at ourselves. This infallible and revolutionary guide from the author of *On Having No Head* – whose work C. S. Lewis described as 'highest genius' – shows how.

Shadows in the Cave Graham Dunstan Martin

We can all recognize our friends in a crowd, so why can't we describe in words what makes a particular face unique? The answer, says Graham Dunstan Martin, is that our minds are not just computers: drawing constantly on a fund of tacit knowledge, we always *know* more than we can ever *say*. Consciousness, in fact, is at the very heart of the universe, and – like the earth itself – we are all aspects of a single universal mind.

The Magus of Strovolos: The Extraordinary World of a Spiritual Healer Kyriacos C. Markides

This vivid account introduces us to the rich and intricate world of Daskalos, the Magus of Strovolos – a true healer who draws upon a seemingly limitless mixture of esoteric teachings, psychology, reincarnation, demonology, cosmology and mysticism, from both East and West.

'This is a really marvellous book . . . one of the most extraordinary accounts of a "magical" personality since Ouspensky's account of Gurdjieff' – Colin Wilson

Meetings With Remarkable Men G. I. Gurdjieff

All that we know of the early life of Gurdjieff – one of the great spiritual masters of this century – is contained within these colourful and profound tales of adventure. The men who influenced his formative years had no claim to fame in the conventional sense; what made them remarkable was the consuming desire they all shared to understand the deepest mysteries of life.

ARKANA – NEW-AGE BOOKS FOR MIND, BODY AND SPIRIT

A selection of titles

On Having No Head: Zen and the Re-Discovery of the Obvious
D. E. Harding

'Reason and imagination and all mental chatter died down . . . I forgot my name, my humanness, my thingness, all that could be called me or mine. Past and future dropped away . . .'

Thus Douglas Harding describes his first experience of headlessness, or no self. This classic work truly conveys the experience that mystics of all ages have tried to put into words.

Self-Healing: My Life and Vision Meir Schneider

Born blind, pronounced incurable – yet at 17 Meir Schneider discovered self-healing techniques which within four years led him to gain a remarkable degree of vision. In the process he discovered an entirely new self-healing system, and an inspirational faith and enthusiasm that helped others heal themselves. While individual response to self-healing is unique, the healing power is inherent in all of us.

'This remarkable story is tonic for everyone who believes in the creative power of the human will' – Marilyn Ferguson.

The Way of the Craftsman: A Search for the Spiritual Essence of Craft Freemasonry W. Kirk MacNulty

This revolutionary book uncovers the Kabbalistic roots of Freemasonry, showing how Kabbalistic symbolism informs all of its central rituals. W. Kirk MacNulty, a Freemason for twenty-five years, reveals how the symbolic structure of the Craft is designed to lead the individual step by step to psychological self-knowledge, while at the same time recognising mankind's fundamental dependence on God.

Arkana Dictionary of Astrology Fred Gettings

Easily accessible yet sufficiently detailed to serve the needs of the practical astrologer, this fascinating reference book offers reliable definitions and clarifications of over 3000 astrological terms, from the post-medieval era to today's most recent developments.

ARKANA – NEW-AGE BOOKS FOR MIND, BODY AND SPIRIT

A selection of titles

Herbal Medicine for Everyone Michael McIntyre

'The doctor treats but nature heals.' With an increasing consciousness of ecology and a move towards holistic treatment, the value of herbal medicine is now being fully recognized. Discussing the history and principles of herbal medicine and its application to a wide range of diseases and ailments, this illuminating book will prove a source of great wisdom.

The Tarot Alfred Douglas

The puzzle of the original meaning and purpose of the Tarot has never been fully resolved. An expert in occult symbolism, Alfred Douglas explores the traditions, myths and religions associated with the cards, investigates their historical, mystical and psychological importance, and shows how to use them for divination.

Views from the Real World G. I. Gurdjieff

Only through self-observation and self-exploration, Gurdjieff asserted, could man develop his consciousness. To this end he evolved exercises through which awareness could be heightened and enlightenment attained. *Views from the Real World* contains his talks and lectures on this theme as he travelled from city to city with his pupils. What emerges is his immensely human approach to self-improvement.

Shape Shifters: Shaman Women in Contemporary Society
Michele Jamal

Shape Shifters profiles 14 shaman women of today – women who, like the shamans of old, have passed through an initiatory crisis and emerged as spiritual leaders empowered to heal the pain of others.

'The shamanic women articulate what is intuitively felt by many "ordinary" women. I think this book has the potential to truly "change a life"' – Dr Jean Shinoda Bolen, author of *Goddesses in Everywoman*